Intimacy After Trauma

of related interest

Gender Trauma

Healing Cultural, Social, and Historical Gendered Trauma

Alex Iantaffi

Foreword by Meg-John Barker

ISBN 978 1 78775 106 4

eISBN 978 1 78775 107 1

Gay Man Talking

All the Conversations We Never Had

Daniel Harding

ISBN 978 1 83997 094 8

eISBN 978 1 83997 095 5

The Go-To Relationship Guide for Gay Men

From Honeymoon to Lasting Commitment

Tom Bruett

ISBN 978 1 80501 265 8

eISBN 978 1 80501 266 5

Intimacy After Trauma

A GUIDE FOR GAY MEN

MICHAEL R. DURYEA

Jessica Kingsley Publishers
London and Philadelphia

First published in Great Britain in 2026 by Jessica Kingsley Publishers
An imprint of John Murray Press

1

Front cover image source: iStockphoto®. The cover image is for illustrative purposes only, and any person featuring is a model.

This book contains mention of physical and emotional abuse, homophobia, transphobia, drug abuse, addiction, suicide, racism, ableism, and transphobia.

A CIP catalogue record for this title is available from the British Library and the Library of Congress

ISBN 978 1 80501 709 7
eISBN 978 1 80501 710 3

Printed and bound in the United States by Integrated Books International

Jessica Kingsley Publishers' policy is to use papers that are natural, renewable and recyclable products and made from wood grown in sustainable forests. The logging and manufacturing processes are expected to conform to the environmental regulations of the country of origin.

Jessica Kingsley Publishers
Carmelite House
50 Victoria Embankment
London EC4Y 0DZ

www.jkp.com

John Murray Press
Part of Hodder & Stoughton Ltd
An Hachette Company

The authorised representative in the EEA is Hachette Ireland,
8 Castlecourt Centre, Dublin 15, D15 XTP3, Ireland (email: info@hbgi.ie)

Contents

Introduction: The Terrain We Tread 11
A shared path into the forest 12
My personal journey 12
Why self-compassion? 13
What makes this book different? 13
Navigating the journey ahead 13
Stepping forward together 15

Chapter 1. Recognizing Relational Trauma: Understanding Your Emotional Wounds 17
Trauma that flies under the radar 18
Two core trauma categories 19
My clinical perspective 20
Acute, chronic, and complex trauma 20
Microaggressions and negative loops 22
Recognizing patterns, choosing a new response 23
Trauma at the intersections 24
The power of resilience 25

Daily awareness instead of formal reflections 25

Your first step toward healing............................ 27

Chapter 2. Facing Unique Challenges: Gay Men's Realities and Resilience.................. 29

Stepping beyond the tree line: from inner wounds to outer terrain.................................... 29

Why stepping outward matters 30

Thorny vines in the underbrush: minority stress 31

Coming out as a lifelong expedition 35

Sheltered groves in the forest: chosen families 39

Navigating the thickets: workplace disclosure............. 42

Intersectionality: your permanent compass............... 44

Dark shadows from broken branches: HIV stigma 46

Clearing a path vs. losing diversity: respectability politics 49

Rocky terrain blocking the path: legal barriers 51

Cultural narratives, historical secrecy, and collective healing .. 53

Exercises.. 55

Emerging from the undergrowth: drawing it all together 59

Your next step forward 60

Chapter 3. Attachment Foundations: Deciphering the Heart's Map 62

Why attachment matters for gay men.................... 62

Understanding attachment theory: a gay-centric overview ... 63

The four main attachment styles......................... 65

Style #1: secure attachment............................. 66

Style #2: anxious-preoccupied attachment................ 68

Style #3: dismissive-avoidant attachment 70
Style #4: fearful-avoidant (disorganized) attachment 72
Typical childhoods for each style 74
Intersectional factors: layering complexity 75
A personal reflection 76
Exercises to deepen self-awareness and adaptation 77
Moving forward: how attachment shapes future chapters in this book 79
Conclusion: mapping a path to healthier bonds 80

Chapter 4. Nurturing the Inner Self: Embracing Self-Compassion and Acceptance.......... 82
A personal reflection 83
Why self-compassion matters for gay men 84
The science behind self-compassion........................ 87
Practical approaches 88
Overcoming common obstacles 92
A structured approach to self-compassion 94
Weaving self-compassion into daily life 95
Tailoring self-compassion by life stage 97
From harsh self-talk to gentle acceptance 99
Conclusion 100

Chapter 5. Rebuilding Trust: Strengthening Relationship Foundations 102
A personal reflection 103
Why trust anchors relationships 105
How trauma erodes trust 106

Trust in action 108
Exercises for strengthening or rebuilding trust. 112
Intersectionality and cultural nuances. 116
Attachment, accountability, and setting boundaries 118
Conclusion: the ongoing quest for trust 119

Chapter 6. Deeper Connection:
The Power of Intimacy and Vulnerability. 122

The shared trek toward openness: recalling the forest path imagery 123
Why intimacy is profoundly healing: the antidote to shame and isolation. 125
Trauma's echoes in closeness. 126
Attachment styles revisited in the realm of intimacy. 127
Emotional intimacy: sharing our inner worlds and going past surface talk. 128
Physical intimacy: from performance to connection 129
Chemsex and porn influences: confronting the quick high and its impact on gay men 130
Potential pitfalls—and how to navigate them 139
Bridging emotional and physical intimacy. 143
Drawing it all together. 147
Small, honest moments as the seeds of true closeness: the ongoing path 150

Chapter 7. Turning Toward Each Other and
Communicating with Care 152

A deeper journey into the forest of dialogue 153

Spotting emotional bids: the small invitations that guide connection 156
Turning toward vs. turning away: choices that accumulate. . . . 157
Emotional safety: the essential canopy over communication . . 159
Dr. John Gottman's "four horsemen:" origins, research, and why they matter 161
Common pitfalls and solutions for day-to-day challenges. 164
Exercises and rituals for lasting change. 166
Larger themes and long-term maintenance 178
Conclusion: cultivating a lifelong dialogue 180

Chapter 8. Emotional Cartography: Discovering Your Partner's Inner World 185
Beyond everyday conversation. 185
A deeper kind of understanding: the transformative power of mapping 186
Bringing emotional cartography into daily life 186
50+ questions for emotional cartography 192
Strategies and scripts for handling resistance 199
Encouraging cultural sensitivity 200
One step closer to a more intimate bond 201
Call to action 201

Chapter 9. Navigating Perpetual Conflicts: Beyond the Thorny Undergrowth. 203
When the same disagreement won't disappear 203
Defining perpetual conflicts and why they matter 204
Looking deeper: connections to deeper identity or past trauma 205

Core strategies for perpetual conflicts 206
Emotional safety and humor: finding the right mix 210
The lifecycle of a perpetual conflict 213
Tracking and celebrating progress: why acknowledgment is crucial 214
Adapting over time 215
Thriving with the thorns still intact 215
Putting these methods into practice 216
Conclusion: beyond the thorns 217

Chapter 10. Moving Forward Together: Crafting Your Shared Future 218
Standing in the clearing of the forest. 218
Celebrating growth: recognizing your own progress 220
Building a future-proof foundation: returning to key tools 221
Balancing individual autonomy and shared dreams 222
Engaging a larger community and intersectionality 223
Revisiting lessons in the face of life's surprises 224
Final words of encouragement. 226
Stepping forward together 227

Resources and Support 229

Bibliography 236

Introduction

The Terrain We Tread

I remember a chilly December evening in Onalaska, Washington—stars glittered overhead, and the tall fir trees seemed to stand guard beneath a silent sky. Inside our home, I could hear the hum of holiday preparations: a gentle chorus of clinking dishes, distant laughter, and the occasional hushed argument. I'd slipped out onto the porch for some quiet air, feeling both pulled toward the cozy glow inside and oddly removed from it. Maybe you've felt that tension too—surrounded by people but unsure whether it's truly safe to be fully seen.

As gay men, that sense of separation can become all too familiar. We learn early that showing "too much"—laughing too loudly, expressing too many soft edges, or straying from expectations—risks judgment or rejection. Such moments lodge themselves within us. Left unexamined, they shape how we see ourselves and how we approach love. If you've ever hesitated to let someone in for fear they'd recoil at what they discover, this book is for you. Together, we'll tend those echoes: revealing their roots, meeting them with kindness, and forging stronger, more authentic bonds in the process.

A shared path into the forest

Imagine a forest path we walk together. Along the way, faint voices from your past might chime in—family who struggled to accept you, childhood friends who teased you, authority figures who made you feel "less than." Maybe you learned to hide key parts of yourself, braced for rejection, or convinced yourself your real self was "too much." It's exhausting to remain on guard, never feeling fully at ease in your own skin.

Our goal here isn't to pretend these scars don't exist. Rather, we'll shine a light on them, seeing each as part of the story that led you here. From frosty holiday memories to painful family dynamics, we'll trace how past wounds may fuel present fears and patterns. Healing rarely follows a tidy straight line. Even so, each small revelation—each time we notice how what once hurt us still impacts us—opens up a deeper sense of belonging.

My personal journey

I grew up among those tall fir trees in Onalaska—surrounded by nature's beauty yet weighed down by strict beliefs and emotional distance. My grandmother's rigid faith magnified my anxiety about being "different," and my early home life was shaped by addiction, tension, and unpredictable silences. Coming out at twenty-one brought both relief and heartbreak: while I finally voiced my truth, I also discovered how easily even heartfelt disclosures could be met with silence.

Over time, I learned that earlier traumas didn't have to map out my future. Therapy helped me replace harsh self-judgment with self-compassion. Where I once expected rejection, I began to find empathy—for myself and for family who hadn't known how to love me fully. That shift changed the way I showed up in relationships, eventually inspiring me to become a marriage and family therapist. In sharing the same tools that guided my own healing, I discovered that I wasn't alone in carrying these echoes—and that true connection is possible when we face, rather than outrun, our pasts.

Why self-compassion?

You might wonder how "being kinder to yourself" can actually reshape your relationships. For gay men weighed down by shame or the fear of not measuring up, self-compassion is more than a fluffy notion: it directly challenges the toxic voices we've absorbed. As we treat ourselves with warmth and patience, we become less defensive, more secure, and more open to the love we once assumed we didn't deserve.

What makes this book different?

Plenty of relationship guides promise transformations but skirt key realities faced by gay men—like microaggressions, family estrangements, the tug-of-war around body image, or the deep importance of chosen families. This book places those experiences at the center, pairing personal stories (including my own) with universal principles tailored to our diverse journeys. I hope to celebrate our common ground while respecting the many ways we each inhabit this identity.

Navigating the journey ahead

You'll find in these pages:

- *Reflective exercises* that help illuminate old beliefs—like mapping your emotional timeline or writing a supportive letter to your younger self.

- *Personal stories* that show how others navigate parallel struggles, so you're reminded you're never alone.
- *Foundational insights* on how past wounds shape present behavior—and how mindful awareness can soften old patterns.

We won't jump straight into a list of fixes. Instead, we'll first spotlight the emotional baggage and beliefs that run beneath the surface, giving you the groundwork to transform shame into self-acceptance. The path may zigzag, but each reflection and "aha" moment can help you move forward with fresh purpose.

In the chapters that follow, we'll begin by examining our shared experiences as gay men—understanding the cultural pressures, traumas, and hidden fears many of us carry (Chapters 1–2). Then we'll dive into how these histories can shape our attachments, influencing the way we handle closeness or conflict (Chapter 3). We'll see why self-compassion forms the bedrock of lasting growth (Chapter 4) before we learn to build trust, deepen intimacy, and manage recurring relationship tensions (Chapters 5–9). Finally, we'll gather all this into a broader vision of resilience, exploring how to nurture a future where you can truly thrive and where your relationships become a source of healing (Chapter 10).

Doing this work isn't just for yourself—it ripples outward. You might model a healthier vulnerability for a younger friend just finding their footing, or shift old dynamics in your chosen family by naming truths that were never spoken aloud. Even seemingly small gestures—comforting a newly out acquaintance, calmly countering a homophobic remark—can spark real change. By nurturing your own roots, you become a more solid presence for those around you.

Stepping forward together

Wherever your personal echoes began, you have the power to outgrow them. I invite you to step into these chapters with a mix of curiosity and courage, honoring your own pace. Maybe old hurts will resurface—if so, hold them gently. And trust in the resilience that brought you here. Healing has both an intimate and communal dimension; sharing what we learn not only strengthens us but also helps others discover their own paths.

Let's walk into this forest prepared to explore, ready to discover a brighter clearing where genuine connection can flourish. Though uncertainty may shadow parts of the trail, you won't face it alone. Together, we'll uncover the strength you've had all along, reshape beliefs that kept you small, and spark a self-worth that stands firm, no matter who you love or where you've come from.

Welcome to this journey. Let's begin.

CHAPTER 1

Recognizing Relational Trauma

Understanding Your Emotional Wounds

Picture a crowded house party, music thumping in the background. Someone's balancing a plate of snacks in one hand and a plastic cup in the other, laughing with a tight-knit circle of friends. You step inside the house, feeling a spark of anticipation—maybe you've been looking forward to this for days—yet a familiar heaviness settles on your shoulders. Your heart picks up speed, and one question surfaces: *Am I really welcome here?*

In an instant, your mind flickers back to a high school cafeteria where peers snickered, or a tense holiday dinner with relatives who never truly acknowledged your orientation. Though the current scene is upbeat on the surface, old echoes of shame or exclusion might color every gesture you make. Whether these echoes arise from a single life-altering blow or from a slow accumulation of smaller wounds, they can linger, shaping how you navigate new connections and experiences. This chapter focuses on identifying those hidden forces and taking the first step toward healing what you may have assumed was irreparable.

Trauma that flies under the radar

We often imagine trauma as an explosive event—some unmistakable crisis. Yet sometimes it's more like a subtle draft under a sealed window: barely visible, but persistent enough to keep you uneasy. Perhaps you catch yourself flinching whenever a loved one says, "We need to talk," or bracing when you realize you're the only gay person in a crowded room. Often, you can't pinpoint precisely why you're tense; your body just sounds the alarm. Over weeks and months, these "minor" alerts can accumulate into a quiet but deeply entrenched sense of caution—reflecting old wounds that never got the chance to heal in the open.

In my early twenties, I worked in an office celebrated for being "friendly" and "diverse," yet casual remarks about "gay drama" or jokes like "He's totally queening out" floated around. Eager not to appear defensive, I laughed politely, insisting it was no big deal. Beneath the surface, though, I started second-guessing my mannerisms, anxious that I might become the next punchline. What seemed trivial to bystanders—"They're just teasing!"—for me created an undercurrent of fear, hinting that even mundane spaces might not be fully safe. Over time, this low-key anxiety piled atop earlier rejections, forming what I eventually recognized as a subtle, ongoing trauma.

When you share discomfort about these "small" moments, others might dismiss it: "They're joking—lighten up." That can reinforce a sense of isolation, as if you're overreacting or lacking humor. In reality, even minor slights add up, particularly if you already bear deeper scars from family or past partners. Each new insult or joke can feel like one more reminder that your real self needs to stay tucked away.

Two core trauma categories

Mental health professionals typically speak of trauma in two broad forms: *acute (isolated) events* and *ongoing (relational) trauma.* Both can shape your sense of worth or emotional safety, though they unfold differently.

Acute (*isolated*) events

Think of a lightning bolt cracking across a clear sky—no warning, just a single electrifying moment that fractures your security. That's an acute trauma: one potent incident that permanently reshapes how safe or valued you feel in the world. Marco's story captures this stark rupture.

> Marco (late thirties, Latino cis gay man) once loved walking home at night after meeting friends—earbuds in, relishing the quiet. Then, a single incident: footsteps closing behind him, an angry voice hissing, "Hey, faggot!" before fists slammed into his ribs. In seconds, his carefree routine ended, replaced by panic and the phrase "You don't belong here" echoing in his mind. Even months later, the slightest noise on a dark street triggered palpitations. A coworker's "Just forget it" only deepened his sense of isolation, trivializing a trauma that altered his life overnight.

Ongoing (*relational*) trauma

Now imagine a slow leak above your ceiling: a drip here, a stain there, seemingly too minor to fret over—until mold takes over and your entire ceiling sags. That's how repeated emotional harm from someone close can wear down your well-being.

Avi (early forties, cis gay man) experienced this in a relationship where his partner erupted over small things—missing groceries, suggesting chore splits—and hurled insults like "You're so useless!" or slammed doors in rage. To keep the peace, Avi tiptoed around every conversation. Even after escaping that dynamic, he noticed a new boyfriend's mild frustration could make his chest tighten, as if bracing for another door slam. Years of repeated insults taught Avi to interpret conflict as catastrophic.

My clinical perspective

In my therapy practice, I've watched how seemingly small childhood slights—"Don't act so gay!"—accumulate on top of heartbreak from an emotionally distant parent. Layer by layer, these experiences often blossom into *complex trauma*, where every new wound reactivates the old ones, reinforcing beliefs like *I'm never enough* or *Everyone leaves eventually.* Spotting these interlocking injuries can unlock the process of unraveling them, transforming a tangled mess of triggers into more identifiable pieces you can address over time.

Acute, chronic, and complex trauma

Beyond the two main categories—acute vs. ongoing trauma—professionals sometimes label traumas more specifically:

- *Acute relational trauma:* A single betrayal (e.g., discovering a supportive parent was covertly pushing you into "conversion therapy").

- *Chronic relational trauma:* The daily drip of criticism, control, or gaslighting from someone you trust.
- *Complex relational trauma:* Multiple distinct traumas across your life—like bullying at school, rejection at home, or emotional abuse from a partner—merging into a deep-seated suspicion of intimacy.

You might see elements of one or all three in your history. Naming the shape of your trauma doesn't trap you; instead, it can validate why certain triggers weigh heavily on you. Maybe you faced that single, life-altering blow, or maybe you have suffered decades of small humiliations chipping away at your self-assurance. Understanding how your experiences align with these patterns can shed light on old reflexes that still color your daily life.

TRAUMATIC RESPONSES

Lior's self-doubt

Lior is a cis gay man in his late thirties. Lior's mother used to say, "I love you, but tone down that prancing," whenever he burst with excitement. Later, a boyfriend rolled his eyes any time Lior got enthusiastic about a new pop album. One evening, at a friend's dinner party, Lior was telling an animated story until his boyfriend whispered, "Calm down—you're making a scene." His cheeks burned as he fell silent, replaying it in bed that night: *I must be too dramatic. I can't do anything right.* Even now, a gentle comment from a new partner—"Maybe phrase that differently"—can send him spiraling into self-criticism.

Marco's lingering alert

Marco once loved nighttime walks. Then came one vicious assault, complete with homophobic slurs and fists driving into his side. He woke in the hospital, hearing well-intentioned but dismissive words: "It's random—just move on." But he couldn't. Months later, the idea of strolling after dark filled him with dread. A passing stranger, a sudden noise—anything could trigger the memory of that hateful voice. "You people don't belong here" echoed in his mind, rewriting how he moved through the world.

Avi's chronic fear

For Avi, it was day after day of emotional whiplash. His partner snapped at trivial issues: "Are you stupid?" "Shut up!" Doors slammed at the smallest conflict. Avi tried to be "good" to avoid these outbursts, stifling his own needs. Years later, in a new, gentler relationship, he still felt that spike of dread whenever his boyfriend calmly said, "We need to talk," as though an eruption loomed. Therapy revealed he'd internalized a perpetual "safety mode." Simply hearing someone's mildly annoyed voice brought back all those slammed doors, feeding the reflex to withdraw before harm arrived.

Microaggressions and negative loops

Not all trauma presents as overt violence or screaming matches. Often, it seeps in through microaggressions—like a coworker's smirk when you mention your partner, or a friend who says, "I'm cool with you being gay, just don't flaunt it." You might curb public affection, change pronouns in casual stories, or avoid referencing certain hobbies that people stereotypically link to being "too gay." Each step might feel minor, but over time, these micro-edits can condition you to see your identity as something to keep in check, reinforcing an undercurrent of shame.

I once worked in a supposedly inclusive setting where people joked about men "queening out," implying flamboyance was fodder for humor. Nobody aimed the jokes directly at me, so I told myself it was harmless. Yet each time, a small part of me tightened, wondering if I'd be next. Over months, that tension built. Eventually, I realized these remarks were microaggressions that undermined my sense of belonging. Validating my own discomfort proved a crucial step in regaining self-trust.

Microaggressions can create loops of self-blame: *Why am I overreacting?* or *I should be tougher*. These mental loops sometimes fuel anxiety or depression, prompting you to either push people away (fearing an inevitable letdown) or tolerate poor treatment (believing you deserve no better). Recognizing them as trauma echoes—rather than objective truths—helps restore your sense of worth. You're not "too sensitive"; you're responding to real harm that others may have overlooked.

Recognizing patterns, choosing a new response

A major pivot in healing emerges when you realize that present-day triggers often replay older pains. Perhaps you freeze if someone raises their voice because your early attempts at self-expression were met with punishment. Or you bristle at a playful tease because it mirrors bullying from your teens.

That moment of insight—*This is my old wound flaring up*—lets you pause and decide how you want to respond. I sometimes compare it to having your phone locked onto a heartbreaking playlist: every message triggers the same sad track. But you can, with mindful effort, switch to a new set of tunes, letting a dash of compassion or humor replace the reflex of shame.

If you're feeling unsettled by how these examples mirror your own history, take a gentle breath. Notice any tension in your shoulders or jaw. Then consider the thought: *I see these old hurts. I'm allowed to feel uneasy.* That quiet acknowledgment can help shift you from helpless reactivity to calm awareness. Even if the discomfort remains, you're no longer swallowed by it. This simple gesture might seem small, but repeated moments of self-validation can gradually reshape your emotional landscape.

Trauma at the intersections

For many gay men, trauma intersects with other identities—race, faith, disability, older age, or trans status. You might be a Latino gay man encountering racism within certain LGBTQ+ spaces and homophobia within your cultural community, compounding the sense of never fully belonging. Or an older gay man whose formative years lacked legal protections or open support systems, carrying lingering wariness of authority or social gatherings. Each additional identity layer can intensify potential triggers, making casual remarks or slight disapproval echo more deeply. Recognizing these overlapping factors underscores why some "small" interactions can sting so sharply—they aren't isolated experiences but part of a broader tapestry of marginalization.

The power of resilience

Trauma might convince you that you're weak or broken, yet a quick glance at your life likely reveals a string of adversities survived. Maybe you came out in a conservative community, faced microaggressions at work but still showed up each day, or rebuilt friendships after heartbreak. Each hardship that you have overcome highlights your adaptability.

> Lior, for instance, found little victories in contradicting the old "too dramatic" refrain, discovering that many circles actually appreciated his lively spirit.

> Daniel (forties, cis gay man) recognized that traveling to his conservative hometown triggered teenage insecurities, and he took proactive steps—staying with supportive friends, setting time limits on family visits.

Such actions illustrate that your past need not define your future. You already hold the seeds of resilience.

Daily awareness instead of formal reflections

Rather than just relying on end-of-week or monthly reflections, consider gently weaving awareness into your daily routine:

- *Spot sudden shame:* If you feel an unexplained jolt of anxiety—maybe reading a text or hearing a coworker's sarcastic comment—ask which older memory or dynamic might be resonating.

- *Pause before reacting:* If you notice yourself snapping at a friend or abruptly withdrawing, question whether it's connected to a deeper wound from your past.
- *Practice self-compassion:* Replace thoughts like *I'm so pathetic* with *I'm hurting, and that's understandable*. Over time, this shift challenges the loop of self-criticism born of past injuries.

If these internal check-ins stir potent memories—like flashbacks, nightmares, or intense despair—professional support can be essential. A qualified therapist, LGBTQ+-affirming counselor, or a community support group can offer tailored guidance, ensuring you don't navigate these uncharted waters alone. See the 'Resources' section at the end of the book for therapist directories and LGBTQ+ community organizations.

Let's return to the scene that opened this chapter: you, standing in the doorway of a lively house party, feeling your breath quicken with a question: *Am I welcome here?* Now that you're more aware of how past traumas might fuel that dread, imagine pausing for a moment. You notice your tightened shoulders and recall how old put-downs once taught you to brace. Then you remind yourself: *This place isn't the old cafeteria or my aunt's judgmental table. I can choose a different way.*

Perhaps you ease into conversation with someone who seems approachable, or you find a friend who offers a brief hug. If an uncomfortable joke arises, you consider how to respond—maybe politely saying "Not cool," or stepping away if it feels safer. Each choice reclaims your power from the reflexes old trauma tried to embed. No, the transformation isn't instant. Your pulse might still spike at certain cues. But each time you recognize the flash of anxiety and consciously decide how to handle it, you weaken the old script that insists *This is dangerous—run or hide!*

Your first step toward healing

We've explored how trauma can emerge from one abrupt blow or a series of smaller injuries—like mild but hurtful jokes or demeaning remarks from authority figures. We've seen how experiences with family, ex-partners, colleagues, or larger societal attitudes can leave echoes that persist in new settings. We've also glimpsed how noticing your triggers can disrupt them, opening space for kindness toward yourself instead of defaulting to shame or panic.

Before you move on to Chapter 2, reflect on your own equivalent of that "house party" scenario—whether it's an actual social event, a work meeting, or a phone call with a relative whose tone unsettles you. The next time you sense that swirl of apprehension, try pausing. Inhale gently, exhale slowly, and think: *This feeling has its roots in old pain, but I can meet it with empathy now.* Even this brief act of naming can shift the dynamic, reminding you that while trauma may have shaped certain reflexes, it doesn't have the final say over your present choices.

In the chapters ahead, you'll gather tools for building trust, handling conflicts without reigniting old fears, fostering emotional and sexual intimacy, and grounding yourself in a healthier self-image. Think of it as continuing along a forest path: you've just noticed the brambles that snag at your clothes, recognized the shadows that make you uneasy. Each step forward leads to a clearing of stronger self-compassion and genuine connection with others. For now, let the final image be you at that threshold: shoulders a touch looser, mind a fraction calmer, aware that your past experiences need not define how you show up in the world today.

Each boundary you set, each honest breath you draw, rewrites part of the script that older traumas tried to inscribe. You are allowed to be here. You are allowed to be yourself. And you are allowed to find the belonging you've long been denied.

CHAPTER 2

Facing Unique Challenges

Gay Men's Realities and Resilience

Stepping beyond the tree line: from inner wounds to outer terrain

This chapter invites you to step gently into a wider landscape. If you've done personal work—identifying trauma, building self-compassion—you might wonder why the external world still matters. Because the environment you move through can either nurture your healing or snag at old wounds. As you read, pace yourself. Each example or story may awaken personal memories; that's okay. Take breaks when needed. You're allowed to rest, reflect, and return at your own comfort level.

In Chapter 1 we focused on internal struggles—traumas, insecurities, and shame that might quietly erode your sense of worth. You can picture that as resting in a sunlit clearing, a space to notice and tend to emotional bruises. Now we step into an expansive forest, encountering tall, ancient trees representing societal barriers, plus thick undergrowth symbolizing everyday jabs like microaggressions. In short, it's not enough to heal yourself in isolation if you keep facing external triggers—families who reject you, workplaces that subtly punish "too much" queerness, or app disclaimers like "No fems." This chapter explores those outer challenges, from minority stress and repeated coming out to chosen families and HIV stigma, culminating in a broader sense of how your environment intersects with your internal journey.

> Daniel once told me: "For years, I thought self-care alone was enough. Then I realized every time I visited my conservative hometown, I felt 16 again—scared and small. It reminded me that *external triggers matter too.*"

Daniel's experience underscores a truth many of us share: inner healing is crucial, but so is acknowledging the realities that can reawaken old fears. So in these pages we'll examine social and cultural forces shaping gay men's lived experiences. Think of it like navigating a forest trail, eyes open for thorny vines or uneven ground. The goal is neither paranoia nor surrender; it's mindful preparedness, letting you find hidden growth and resilience where you might least expect them.

Why stepping outward matters

"I've done therapy; I'm learning self-compassion—so why worry about ignorance or laws?" Because if your environment constantly chips at your worth, no amount of inner affirmation can flourish unchallenged. Minor or major, these external stressors can retrigger old wounds. For trans gay men, that interplay can intensify if certain gay spaces erase or misunderstand trans identities, leading to double scrutiny.

We'll explore how public attitudes, family pressures, or

workplace bias can complicate the journey you began in Chapter 1. For instance, a father who refuses to learn your new name and pronouns can undermine your self-esteem, or a boss who jokes about "masc guys only" might sap the confidence you've painstakingly built. By identifying these external forces—like old brambles in the forest—you can combine your inner work with boundary-setting, resource-finding, or activism, ensuring you're not trying to heal in a vacuum.

Thorny vines in the underbrush: minority stress

Defining those tangled vines

Minority stress, first conceptualized by Dr. Ilan H. Meyer (2003), refers to the *added weight* that people in marginalized groups carry because of prejudice and the persistent worry of rejection or hostility. It's like creeping vines clinging to your ankles each time you venture into new territory:

> You show up at a workplace or social event wondering if subtle homophobia lurks.
>
> You board a bus or train, scanning for glares at you and your partner holding hands.
>
> You debate how to explain being trans to an acquaintance who may—or may not—be open-minded.

Over weeks, months, or years, this vigilance can coil around your sense of safety, leading to self-censorship or constant bracing.

> Jeremy (late twenties, trans gay man) recalls wearing headphones constantly "to block out strangers' comments," effectively shutting out the world to protect himself.

The toll of minority stress

That's the cost of minority stress: mental and emotional energy spent not on thriving, but on *fending off potential harm*. Studies published in the *American Journal of Community Psychology* (for example, Frost & Meyer, 2009) show that ongoing, low-grade vigilance can elevate stress-related health problems (like high blood pressure or tension headaches) and fuel emotional struggles (like anxiety, depression, or self-doubt) (see, for example, Frost and Meyer 2009; Meyer 2003). Across time, minority stress chips away at your sense of ease, shaping how you behave in friendships, romantic bonds, or family gatherings. It's not that you're "too sensitive"—it's that you've internalized the need to be on guard, never sure when rejection might strike.

Where these vines of minority stress show up

Dating—apps and real life

On dating apps, disclaimers like "No fems" or "No trans" can feel like a thousand tiny slaps, echoing: "You're not wanted here unless you fit a narrow mold." In bars or social gatherings, someone might ask prying questions about your anatomy or assume you "pass" or hide certain traits. If this repeats often, it's easy to question whether you're acceptable as you are.

Family and home life

An older relative might say, "We're okay with you being gay, but don't make it a big deal." Or a cousin might shrug when you mention your partner, implying discomfort. If you're trans, a relative might refuse your chosen name, brushing it off as "a phase." Each remark can sow doubt about whether you truly belong in your own family.

Public spaces

Holding hands with your boyfriend, or hugging after dinner, can trigger self-conscious scanning: *Is this safe? Will someone glare or comment?* If you're trans, a casual outing can become fraught—restroom usage alone can spur confrontation or stares.

Small-town or rural workplaces

In smaller communities, the workplace can feel like an extended family if colleagues are open-minded. But if they're not, your life can become a fishbowl. Gossip spreads fast if you break local "norms." If you're from a marginalized racial or cultural group on top of being gay or trans, you might face overlapping biases.

> Ron (twenties, cis gay man): "Seeing 'Masc only' in profiles makes me question if I'm manly enough—exhausting."

> Derek (thirties, trans man): "Every Thanksgiving, my mother uses my old name, saying she can't adapt. It cuts deeper than she'll ever know."

THEO'S MONTHLY RETURN

Theo (thirties, cis gay man) drives three hours each month to see family in a conservative hometown. Stepping out of the car, tension tightens his neck. Neighbors greet him with polite confusion—"When do we see you with a nice girl?" He feels transported back to awkward adolescence, uncertain whether to correct them or quietly endure. The dread leaves him emotionally spent, echoing that sense of minority stress weighing on his day-to-day life.

Trimming the vines: coping techniques

- *Grounding in a mental clearing:* If you sense tension at a co-worker's sly remark, mentally step into a calm scene, maybe from a favorite memory. Then remind yourself: *Their bias isn't my identity*.
- *Seeking supportive companions:* Online or in-person meetups—like local LGBTQ+ groups—offer spaces where you can vent about microaggressions and affirm each other's experiences.
- *Mapping patterns:* Keep a short journal of each slight or microaggression for two weeks, noting context. Do certain times, places, or people cause repeated stress? Identifying patterns helps you decide if boundary-setting, a chat with HR, or skipping certain events is the best step.
- *Balancing action and avoidance:* Some days, you might address a rude joke directly—"I'm not okay with that." Other times, you might walk away or lean on a friend's support. Let your intuition guide when to engage or conserve energy.

You *aren't obligated* to educate every ignorant person. Sometimes stepping aside is an act of self-care; other times, speaking up feels liberating. There's no universal rule—listen to your gut about which moments warrant confrontation and which require a graceful exit.

Reflection: Which domain—dating, family, workplace, or public spaces—feels most tangled for you? Do any specific incidents still weigh on you, making your body tighten or breath shorten? Recognizing these vines as external stressors, not personal failings, can ease self-blame. Minority stress doesn't make you weak; it highlights a world still rife with prejudice. Even so, you deserve both internal and community-based strategies to protect your well-being.

Coming out as a lifelong expedition

Shattering the "one and done" myth

Popular culture often frames coming out as a single, triumphant moment—like a big reveal at eighteen or on social media, followed by total relief. Realistically, you face multiple coming-out junctures: a new job, an unfamiliar friend circle, or even a doctor's office. Each setting can trigger the question: *Is it safe to be transparent?* That can be both freeing (if you find acceptance) and draining (if you fear rejection).

Jamal (twenties, cis gay man): "I came out at eighteen, but each time I start somewhere new, it's back to the closet until I sense if they're cool with it."

For trans gay men, this may double: you might pass as a cis man, so do you share your trans history? Are certain details private or necessary? Deciding repeatedly how much to disclose can be exhausting, yet also can be a chance to claim your truth in diverse spaces.

Different ages, different challenges

Young adulthood (teens/early twenties)

Social media can help you find peer support swiftly but also invites bullying or forced outings. You might still live with a family who disapprove, risking eviction or emotional harm.

> One teen, Evan (nineteen, cis gay man), posted a Pride picture. An aunt screenshotted it and forwarded it to his parents, effectively outing him overnight. He felt exposed and betrayed, yet also freed from secrecy.

Thirties/forties

Career concerns can loom large; you might wonder if being out curtails promotions or shifts coworker perceptions. Family obligations might weigh on you: parents might sidestep your identity or hush you at gatherings. If you're a trans gay man, you might field repeated questions like, "Wait, so you like men?"

> Victor (thirties, cis gay man): "I'm out at home, not at work. I can't shake the fear my boss will see me differently."

Later life (fifties, sixties, and beyond)

Some older men were married heterosexually for decades, coming out only post-divorce or after a conservative parent passed away. Others may have been out for years but face ageism in younger gay crowds. A trans man might hear, "Why bother transitioning now? Aren't you set in your ways?"

> Leo (sixties, cis gay man) observes: "I'm newly exploring the gay community. Sometimes I feel I missed the boat, but every day I remind myself it's never too late to be who you truly are."

Asexual and graysexual trails[1]

Some gay men identify as *asexual* (no sexual attraction) or *graysexual* (rare or context-dependent desire), challenging the stereotype that gay male culture is endlessly sexual. People might question, "How do you know you're gay if you rarely want sex?" This invalidation can feel isolating. Searching out specialized groups or platforms can confirm you're not alone.

> Tristan (twenties, graysexual) felt uneasy with the constant sexual banter on apps. After stumbling on a graysexual online forum, he realized he wasn't just "repressed"—he

1 For direct links to asexual/graysexual support, the Asexual Visibility & Education Network (AVEN) offers forums and resources for all forms of asexual and graysexual identities (www.asexuality.org). Some LGBTQ+ centers host meetups for less-common orientations—check local listings or ask staff about specialized groups.

was simply wired differently. That sense of solidarity replaced the self-doubt that once haunted him.

ZACH'S MIDLIFE REVELATION

Zach (fifties, cis gay man) spent decades in a "safe" heterosexual marriage, even though he realized he was gay in his twenties. By fifty-seven, post-divorce, he finally walked into a gay bar. It felt like stepping onto another planet—young men used slang he'd never heard, and dating apps mystified him. Initially, he felt discouraged, wondering if he'd waited too long. Then he found an "Older Gay Men's Circle" at a community center. Through casual potlucks, shared stories about coming out, and intergenerational meetups, Zach bridged the gap. He discovered that while dating norms had shifted over the years, empathy and friendship transcended those differences. What began as disorientation turned into a supportive new chapter, showing it's never too late to embrace authenticity.

Steps for each "clearing"

- *Young adulthood (teens/early twenties:* Seek youth-centric LGBTQ+ groups, safe shelters if needed, or online communities that validate young experiences. If forced out or at risk, reach out to crisis lines or supportive adults. (See the Resources at the end of the book.)
- *Thirties/forties:* Consider drafting a plan for workplace or

family disclosure—perhaps rehearsing how you'll address it. Gather allies for emotional backup.

- *Later life (fifties, sixties, and beyond):* Don't underestimate bridging generation gaps. Many younger LGBTQ+ people value older perspectives. Look for "Over fifty" or "Intergenerational" community groups.

- *Asexual/graysexual and multiple layers:* Besides therapy or peer support, exploring specific networks can help. Online forums (e.g., AVEN) or local gatherings might offer the perfect niche for your orientation and identity.

Gentle reassurance: You can come out selectively or keep some details private; there's no universal script for living openly. Whether you reveal your orientation, trans history, or other facets at eighteen or eighty, it's valid. Trust your pace and context.

Sheltered groves in the forest: chosen families

The sanctuary of chosen kin

Sometimes our biological families can't—or won't—meet our emotional and practical needs. This lack of acceptance can feel devastating. But in many LGBTQ+ communities, a "chosen family" emerges as a refuge: close friends, mentors, housemates, or even ex-partners who provide genuine care without the usual "shoulds" or conditions. Think of it as a sheltered grove within the larger forest, a circle of protective trees that stands strong against external storms.

For instance, a Deaf trans gay man rejected by relatives might find genuine belonging in a small friend group that accommodates sign language, respects his name and pronouns, and celebrates his life milestones. Or a middle-aged gay couple might welcome younger men who've been disowned, creating a patchwork family that shares meals, holidays, and mutual support. The key is genuine solidarity: everyone is there by choice, united by empathy rather than blood ties.

Why chosen families matter—and how they form

A chosen family can evolve organically—like a group of friends who start having regular game nights—or more deliberately, when people sense a shared void and decide to fill it collectively. For example, in a city with scarce acceptance, a few queer neighbors might coordinate monthly potlucks, building trust through consistent warmth. Over time, they transform from casual acquaintances to each other's emergency contacts, holiday hosts, and emotional anchors.

KEVIN'S EXTENDED HOUSEHOLD

Kevin (thirties, cis gay man) found four like-minded gay men in his building. They began splitting rent, chores, and late-night chats. Soon, they launched a "Hearts and Concerns" ritual each month, giving each housemate 10–15 minutes to air their joys or annoyances. One member was trans, and the others stood up for him when misgendering relatives visited, helped him research medical transitions, and never let cultural ignorance slide. This household transcended typical roommate arrangements—becoming a genuine chosen family that addressed everything from shared dinners to deeper heartbreaks.

Strengthening your chosen family

It might sound simple—"Just gather friends!"—but forming a real chosen family can be more nuanced. Friends may not all know each other, or they might bring different communication styles and triggers. So how do you start?

- *Identify potential members:* Consider three to five people who truly "get" you—maybe they've shown up for you in a crisis or embraced your identity wholeheartedly.
- *Propose gatherings:* Suggest monthly or bi-weekly dinners or video calls. If these people don't all know each other, begin with casual events: simple potlucks, board games, or watch parties to ease them into a shared space.
- *Build trust gradually:* If conflicts arise—someone repeatedly arrives late or makes offhand comments about another's orientation—initiate open dialogue. A gentle "house meeting" or supportive group text can air grievances and avoid buried resentments.
- *Consider formal steps:* Down the line, if you trust them deeply, legal actions like co-owning property or naming each other in healthcare directives might formalize that chosen kinship. Some pick one "house leader" or rotate roles to handle bigger decisions.

Realistically, forging this sense of family might take months or years. It isn't always instant. People have different comfort zones about emotional openness. But if you keep a spirit of empathy, curiosity, and patience, those friendships can deepen into something that functions like family—unconditional acceptance, daily practical help, and unwavering emotional support.

Navigating the thickets: workplace disclosure

Professional norms

Most of us spend a significant chunk of our lives at work. Deciding how "out" to be can raise big questions: *Will my boss judge me? Will my coworkers gossip?* If you're trans, will you face issues around old documents or pronouns? Even in offices that flaunt rainbow logos, managers might penalize employees for being "too flamboyant." Subtler biases can lurk behind official "Diversity & Inclusion" slogans.

> Allan (mid-twenties, cis gay man) shared how one casual mention of "my boyfriend" led his boss to abruptly switch subjects, leaving him feeling shutdown. Over time, such micro-closings can add up, making you wonder if your orientation or identity isn't truly welcome.

Differing environments and intersections

- *Urban corporate:* You might see official Pride floats or Employee Resource Groups (ERGs), but a direct supervisor could still sideline "too out" employees. HR might be supportive of the LGBTQ+ community in theory, but unprepared for trans-specific updates like name changes or pronoun usage.
- *Small-town or rural settings:* Colleagues can feel like a close-knit family if they're accepting. But if they're not, it becomes a fishbowl—everyone knows your personal life. Breaking local norms might spark gossip or subtle ostracism.

- *Multiple marginalizations at work:* A Deaf Black trans gay man might juggle multiple layers of bias—colleagues ignoring sign language accommodations, racist assumptions, or ignorant remarks about trans bodies. A gay man with a visible disability may notice that coworkers treat him with pity, overshadowing his actual skills.

Facing microaggressions and silencing

Seemingly small remarks like, "This is a professional setting, so no personal talk, please" can translate to "We'd rather not hear about your partner or trans journey." Or "You don't look trans" might be framed as a compliment but implies ignorance of trans realities. To cope, you might limit references to your personal life, draining emotional energy you could devote to better things.

Carving your own path

- *Office allies:* Pinpoint at least one coworker who openly supports you. This ally can back you up if inappropriate jokes arise or join you in speaking to HR about inclusive changes.
- *Employee resource groups:* If your workplace has an LGBTQ+ ERG, get involved or help start one. Collective voices often shift culture faster than solo efforts.
- *Documenting incidents:* If you endure repeated jokes, misgendering, or hostility, keep a brief log of dates and what was said. If you pursue official action, such records help ensure you're taken seriously.

Reflection and encouragement: Rate your current workplace (or prospective one) on a scale of 1–10 for genuine, day-to-day inclusivity (where 1 = actively hostile or performative and 10 = deeply inclusive and affirming in everyday practice). If you sense open hostility, you deserve better. Sometimes seeking a more welcoming environment or contacting external support groups might be key to protecting your mental health. Remember, *you're not alone*; many gay and trans people navigate these tensions. By setting small boundaries or finding supportive colleagues, you carve a path for yourself—and potentially open doors for the next LGBTQ+ hire as well.

Intersectionality: your permanent compass

Seeing the forest with multiple layers

We don't hold a single label. If you're a Latino trans gay man, you may confront racism in predominantly white gay spaces, transphobia in mainstream settings, and homophobia within parts of your cultural community. That's intersectionality in action: each identity can magnify the other's challenges, leaving you caught between multiple worlds.

> Darryla (twenties, Black Deaf gay man) recalled blaming himself for never blending in. Then he realized every "circle" lacked accommodations or acceptance for at least one aspect of who he was. Recognizing it wasn't his failing, but a societal gap, proved liberating.

CHALLENGES IN THE WORKPLACE

Marcel's workplace journey

Marcel (thirties, Deaf cis gay man and an immigrant from Belgium) struggled in a trendy gay bar where loud music and dim lighting made signing with Deaf friends nearly impossible. At his day job, some coworkers displayed "ally" stickers but never bothered to adapt communication or even learn basic sign language. Marcel felt as if each "helpful" environment only recognized a fraction of him. Over time, he sought Deaf-friendly social events and found a Deaf gay men's online forum, forging a space where his Deafness, orientation, and immigrant background were all seen as normal, not exotic.

Aaliyah's faith conflicts

Aaliyah (late twenties, trans man primarily attracted to men) grew up in a devout faith community that saw both his trans identity and his queerness as sinful. Even after moving to a more liberal city, he discovered certain gay circles doubted his "realness" as a man who desired men. Meanwhile, his family used his female name in holiday newsletters—"We pray for her confusion." Aaliyah joined a trans men's support group, found a progressive spiritual community, and gradually built his own "middle ground." Each new friend or mentor respected his entire self, bridging his faith roots with his identity in a holistic way.

Strategies for handling intersectional layers

- *Seek specialized spaces:* Deaf gay men's events, trans men's group meets, or older men-of-color gatherings help reduce that "I'm alone" feeling.
- *Join allies in mainstream forums:* In bigger Pride committees or community boards, push for sign language interpreters, highlight men of color, or underscore trans men's medical needs. Collaboration eases the burden of doing it all yourself.
- *Intersectional self-care:* Journal about how each aspect of your identity shapes your day. Plan restful downtime or therapy, mindful of the extra stress each identity can bring.

Reflection prompt: Which part(s) of your identity do mainstream gay spaces overlook—or outright conflict with? Is there an online group or in-person meetup that centers your specific combination of backgrounds? Craving such a space isn't about excluding others; it's about existing without having to fragment who you are.

Dark shadows from broken branches: HIV stigma

Historical crises, lingering wounds

Many older gay men bear the scars of the 1980s–90s AIDS crisis, when the government was slow to act and the media painted gay men as vectors of disease. Younger men may lack that grim history but still encounter stigma or casual ignorance about HIV.

Nathan (forties, cis gay man) recounts losing close friends decades ago. Even though he knows about modern PrEP and U=U, a part of him still sees sex as potentially lethal. Those emotional scars don't disappear just because science has advanced.

U=U and PrEP: doing the homework

- *U=U (Undetectable = Untransmittable):* Maintaining an undetectable viral load through effective meds means zero risk of sexual HIV transmission. This fosters relief for positive men, challenging old narratives of danger or shame.
- *PrEP (pre-exposure prophylaxis):* For HIV-negative men, daily or on-demand PrEP drastically reduces infection risk. Yet misconceptions linger: "If you're on PrEP, you must sleep around." This moralizing can perpetuate stigma and misinformation.

Ben (late twenties, cis gay man) confides that telling a new date he's on PrEP sometimes draws assumptions of promiscuity. In reality, he's simply proactive about sexual health. Understanding these facts can transform fear into confidence, bridging the gap between ignorance and acceptance.

HIV AND AIDS

Kofi's disclosure dilemma

Kofi (thirties, cis gay man), tested HIV-positive at 29. Initially, he felt uprooted—"Does anyone want me now?" He soon achieved an undetectable viral load, meaning no transmission risk, but each new date revived old nerves: when or how to disclose? Some men ghosted him the second he revealed his status; others listened calmly and offered acceptance. Over time, Kofi joined an HIV support group, learning about others' experiences with U=U. Bolstered by real success stories, he opened up more confidently. While rejections still stung, the sense of self-blame lessened, replaced by clarity that his status didn't define his desirability.

Nathan's generational bridge

Nathan (forties, cis gay man) survived the AIDS crisis, losing close friends in the early 1990s. He carried that trauma into modern gay scenes where younger men didn't grasp the heaviness of that era. Some teased him for insisting on condoms or caution, calling him "paranoid." Nathan tried explaining the heartbreak he'd witnessed. Gradually, a few younger friends understood, acknowledging that while medicine had changed, his lived fear remained valid. He now fosters cross-generational discussions, helping men see HIV not just as a clinical issue but also a deeply emotional one.

Coping with HIV stigma

- *Accurate knowledge:* If you're HIV-positive, learn the nuances of U=U. If you're negative, stay open to a partner's positive status, aware they might be undetectable and pose zero risk.
- *Disclosure scripts:* Practice calmly stating, "My viral load is undetectable, so there's no transmission risk," or "I'm on PrEP to protect both of us."
- *Community ties:* Local HIV nonprofits or trans health alliances can provide cutting-edge information, moral support, and solidarity.
- *Reassurance:* HIV no longer precludes love or a fulfilling sex life. Each honest conversation challenges old stigma. Embrace facts and empathy over fear.

Clearing a path vs. losing diversity: respectability politics

Respectability politics means feeling pressure to appear "less gay," "less trans," or "less flamboyant," believing conformity might shield you from discrimination. Maybe you limit public affection around extended family, or pretend you're just "buddies" with your boyfriend to keep the peace. Although it can smooth certain interactions, it can also stifle the vibrant truth of who you are.

> Ellis (late twenties, cis gay man) confesses how he wore a plain suit at his wedding—"I toned down everything to

appease my conservative relatives, but it felt like burying a piece of me." That tension underscores the tradeoff: fitting in might soften external friction, yet it can create internal conflict if you're hiding an important aspect of yourself.

Here are some common examples of respectability politics:

- *Big life milestones, like weddings:* One partner wants a formal, traditional ceremony; the other craves a drag performance or flamboyant touches. They clash over how "out there" to be.
- *Speech, language, and use of slang:* Some people may deliberately minimize queer slang popular in online spaces when they speak, to distance themselves from stereotypes, or try to modulate the pitch of their voice to appear more typically masculine.
- *Clothes, makeup, and self-expression:* One partner might be far more gender nonconforming in their dress and self-expression and the other more traditional. This might cause anxieties around visible queerness in public spaces.

Weighing the costs and benefits

- *Possible upsides:* If you truly prefer a low-key style, you're not betraying yourself by choosing subtlety. Some folks find comfort in privacy.
- *Pitfalls:* If you're editing yourself out of fear or a need to placate others, you may gather resentment or lose your unique spark. Over time, that can damage your self-esteem.

Soft reflection: Where am I aligning with "respectable" norms from genuine choice vs. leftover shame? Could I experiment with a small, more authentic expression in a safe context?

You get to decide your blend of outspokenness vs. privacy. Safety concerns are valid, but so is the desire to show up fully. If certain loved ones will never truly accept you, maybe toning yourself down for them isn't worth the cost. You can also make a separation between your self-expression in the workplace and in your personal life, if you feel more comfortable. Balancing these nuances is deeply personal.

Rocky terrain blocking the path: legal barriers

Overview of the legal hurdles

Even if same-sex marriage is allowed where you live, adoption might remain challenging, or healthcare decision-making rights could be murky. For trans gay men, outdated IDs or birth certificates may cause confusion or denial of services, especially in emergency hospital settings. Seeking accurate legal documents becomes crucial to avoid bureaucratic nightmares.

> Raj (forties, cis gay man) shares how he and his husband married, only to learn that local adoption agencies applied extra scrutiny to gay couples. Polite rejections or endless paperwork confirmed that the law's wording wasn't the only barrier; agency biases also played a role.

Deeper glimpses: adoption, immigration, healthcare

- *Adoption:* Some agencies require "proof" that gay or trans parents can offer a stable household, perpetuating harmful assumptions.
- *Immigration:* Bi-national couples face interviews proving their relationship is "genuine," complicated further if one partner has changed names or gender markers.
- *Healthcare directives:* Without formal paperwork, a hospital might exclude you from your partner's intensive care unit (ICU) room, defaulting to estranged biological relatives for decisions.

RAJ AND MATEO'S LONG ROAD

Raj and Mateo (forties, cis gay men) faced multiple closed doors trying to adopt. A lawyer finally advised moving to a more LGBTQ+-friendly city. Selling their old home, leaving supportive neighbors, and starting anew took an emotional and financial toll. Eventually, they adopted a three-year-old. But the journey was dotted with heartbreak.

Climbing over the legal obstacles

- *LGBTQ+-savvy lawyers:* Seek attorneys specializing in spousal benefits, second-parent adoption, or trans name changes.
- *Activism:* Align with local nonprofits or advocacy groups pushing for inclusive policies. Collective voices often spark broader change.

- *Protective documents:* Consider living wills, co-parent agreements, or healthcare proxies naming your partner. Each step spares massive complications later.

Comforting note: Yes, it can feel overwhelming, but each piece of legal prep helps anchor your rights and security.[2]

Cultural narratives, historical secrecy, and collective healing

Aftermath of historical secrecy

Older generations grew up in times where being openly gay was risky or even criminal, so entire chapters of their lives were shrouded in secrecy. Younger gay men might inherit that secrecy in subtler ways: "We accept it, but let's not talk about it." If you're trans and gay, even supportive relatives might say, "We can handle you being gay, but your transition is too much." The result is a lingering code of silence that fosters emotional distance.

> Adam (mid-thirties, cis gay man) recalls his dad continually changing the subject whenever Adam alluded to a boyfriend: "It's like we have this invisible wall—one I wish he'd let down."

2 Organizations exist specifically for LGBTQ+ legal support—ask local centers or check national resources like Lambda Legal (https://lambdalegal.org) or the ACLU (American Civil Liberties Union) (www.aclu.org).

Digital realities: a mixed bag

- *Social media:* A Pride selfie can gather hearts and supportive comments, but can also out you unexpectedly to extended relatives or homophobic trolls.
- *Dating apps:* Quick connections might lead to deeper bonds or casual fun. Yet disclaimers like "No Asians," "No trans," or fetishizing remarks can remind you that acceptance isn't guaranteed. A trans gay man might weigh disclosing transition details in the bio or waiting for trust to build.

Tapping into communal growth

- *Local LGBTQ+ centers* often run therapy groups or host socials for subcommunities: older gay men, gay men with disabilities, trans men, men of color. In these gatherings, you hear "Me too," dissolving isolation.
- *Online support:* Private online groups, Discord servers, or specialized subreddits provide 24/7 safe spaces for discussing issues like coming out late, dealing with religious shame, or adopting as a gay couple. Realizing others share your struggles can reduce the sense that you're alone.

Leon (twenties, cis gay man) says: "I joined a Slack channel specifically for trans gay men. I saw couples thriving, men discussing hormones, and realized I wasn't some odd outlier."

Reflection: Consider where secrecy still rules in your life. Do you minimize orientation details around certain folks, or hide your trans status from childhood friends? Could you open one small door—maybe telling a trusted cousin about your partner, or mentioning your pronouns to a supportive coworker—if you feel safe?

Gentle encouragement: Letting in a little more light, even in small ways, can create space for deeper self-acceptance. Choose which doors to open and when. Let safety and self-determination guide you.

Exercises

Here is an integrated toolkit referencing everything from *minority stress* to *respectability politics*. Choose whichever resonates most with your current struggles; you don't have to do them all.

MINORITY STRESS "VINE TRACKER"

Time frame: 2–3 weeks.

Process: Note each moment of tension related to your orientation or trans status—like a coworker's slur, a family member's coldness, or an app's disclaimers.

Goal: Spot recurring triggers so you can plan solutions (e.g., talking to HR, boundary-setting, or skipping certain events).

Optional twist: Track your physical responses (tight shoulders, held breath) to see the tangible toll.

COMING OUT LIFE MAP + EMOTIONAL COLOR CODE

Draw a timeline from childhood to today. Mark significant coming-out points. Use *colors*—e.g., green for supportive, red for negative, yellow for neutral.

Look for patterns: do negative experiences cluster around certain people or phases? Recognizing these helps you see where you might want new support or closure.

CHOSEN FAMILY BUILDER

Identify three to five individuals who truly value you.

Host small gatherings (dinners, virtual calls) regularly. If they don't know each other, start with casual get-togethers so they bond organically.

Encourage openness: If conflict arises—e.g., over finances, personal remarks—model open, caring discussion. Not everyone is used to direct talk, so adapt gently.

Deepen over time: Eventually, you might decide to share bigger responsibilities or sign legal documents, if that suits your trust level.

Pro tip: Some city-based LGBTQ+ centers host "Chosen Family Mixers" to connect people seeking a stable friend network. If nothing local exists, consider organizing one yourself. Real bonds take time, but consistent warmth and reliability can spark meaningful kinship.

WORKPLACE CLIMATE AUDIT

Rate your workplace from 1–10 for genuine inclusivity (beyond rainbow logos), where 1 = performative or tokenizing and 10 = deeply embedded, lived inclusion.

Observe if any coworker consistently supports you or if certain individuals often slip into microaggressions.

Plan a small "authenticity test"—like referencing your orientation in passing, or clarifying your pronouns, to gauge real reactions.

If your workplace is hostile: Recognize you deserve an environment that doesn't undermine your identity. Gathering documentation or seeking an LGBTQ+-friendly job can protect your mental health.

INTERSECTIONALITY JOURNAL

Each day for a month, jot down how race, orientation, disability, or trans status shaped an interaction. Afterward, note which spaces felt welcoming. If negative patterns surface—like repeated microaggressions—explore specialized communities or address issues with supportive leaders. Awareness fosters targeted action.

HIV KNOWLEDGE AND STIGMA SHIFT

Self-assessment: Rate your grasp of U=U, PrEP, or local disclosure laws from 1–10, where 1 = no understanding or awareness and 10 = deep, confident knowledge and ability to explain to others.

Communication: If you are HIV-positive, practice calm disclosure scripts. If you are negative, think how you'd respond if a partner shared an HIV-positive status.

Join or contact an HIV-focused group (like GMHC (Gay Men's Health Collective) or local LGBTQ+ health organizations for the latest resources. (See the Resources at the end of the book.)

RESPECTABILITY ALIGNMENT

List the ways you tone down your orientation, expression, or trans identity for "acceptance."

Examine: Which steps are genuine personal preferences vs. attempts to mollify bigotry?

Try a small experiment with letting your real self show in a safe circle. Notice if the worst you feared actually happens.

LEGAL PREP ESSENTIALS

Research local adoption, spousal rights, healthcare directives, and name change laws.

Consult an LGBTQ+-friendly lawyer or nonprofit for detailed guidance.

Draft relevant documents (wills, living wills, co-parenting agreements) proactively. Less stress arises when critical matters are settled in advance.

Pick just one exercise that speaks to you. There is no need to tackle everything immediately. The path is yours to shape.

Emerging from the undergrowth: drawing it all together

The forest's complexity: reflecting gay and trans realities

Throughout this chapter, we saw how personal well-being is intertwined with social realities: microaggressions, repeated coming-out demands, chosen vs. biological families, HIV stigma, respectability politics, intersectional identities, and legal barriers. Recognizing these external factors clarifies why you might think, *Why am I not over this yet?* or *Why do new obstacles keep appearing?* The forest you traverse wasn't planted by you. Some corners remain riddled with prejudice or ignorance.

Returning to internal work

Remember Chapter 1? Healing your internal wounds, naming triggers, and building self-compassion. Yet these external triggers—like a father refusing your gay identity or a workplace that hushes your personal life—can reopen old scars. Naming such outer forces allows you to integrate your internal growth with strategic action (setting boundaries, finding support networks, or even pursuing legal recourse). If you're trans, each external stand (such as insisting on correct pronouns at work) can reinforce your internal self-worth.

Seeds of hope and growth

Yes, challenges exist. But so do pockets of acceptance sprouting everywhere: more workplaces adopting genuine (not just token) policies, more community groups bridging age and race divides, more online spaces for trans men or disabled gay men. These incremental changes expand your scope of possibility.

> Leon (mid-twenties, trans gay man) recalls thinking no cis gay man would date him. Then he joined a trans men's meetup and saw trans-cis couples thriving, rewriting his sense of what was possible. Activists, communities, and everyday folks sharing their stories help rewrite old narratives of invisibility or hopelessness.

Your next step forward

Decide which external stressor feels most pressing. Could it be repeated microaggressions at work? Or family secrecy that exhausts you? Maybe it's the maze of adoption laws or your fear of HIV stigma. Turn to one exercise from this chapter—like the "Minority stress 'vine tracker'" or the "Chosen family builder." Each small action or boundary set can ease the burden, aligning with the inner resilience you nurtured in Chapter 1.

Place a hand on your chest, inhale softly, and exhale with a hint of relief. You've trekked through a dense exploration of external obstacles—barbed vines of prejudice, hush in families, workplace challenges, or legal tangles. If it feels heavy, that's normal. Let yourself pause, remembering that you didn't create these barriers; society did. Yet each boundary you cross or ally you connect with can lighten the load. You have the right to shape your environment as best you can or seek spaces that honor who you are.

Looking ahead to Chapter 3, we'll explore how attachment styles and intimacy intersect with these external pressures. Keep the forest metaphor in mind: your internal clearing from Chapter 1 remains vital, but so is learning to navigate a world still catching up to your fullness. Each boundary, each chosen family tie, each respectful workplace shift affirms that you're carving a more welcoming trail—for yourself and anyone who follows. Small steps can spark wider change, anchored by the knowledge that you deserve acceptance and ease, exactly as you are.

CHAPTER 3

Attachment Foundations

Deciphering the Heart's Map

We've ventured through dense terrain in the previous chapters—examining personal traumas and grappling with a world that doesn't always welcome gay men with open arms. Now, we find ourselves in a more peaceful, sunlit glade of our metaphorical forest, pausing to understand how we bond with others in spite of, or perhaps because of, what we've survived. In this clearing, we focus on *attachment*—the emotional compass that guides how we seek closeness, handle conflict, and respond to love. When we understand the attachment style we developed from childhood, we can reshape our adult relationships with more empathy, clarity, and self-compassion.

Why attachment matters for gay men

The forest's deeper trails

Attachment theory, as originally outlined by John Bowlby (1988) and expanded on by Mary Ainsworth (Salter Ainsworth *et al.* 1978), explains why some of us trust easily and others flinch from closeness. It also shows why some repeatedly latch on to a partner for fear they'll be left behind, and why others alternate between wanting love and pushing it away in panic. For gay men, these patterns rarely unfold in a benign setting. We have grown up in a broader cultural forest that might have had "warning signs" about how "real men" behave, or condemnation from relatives who told us we were sinful or "going through a phase." Trans gay men may face even more complex obstacles—partly accepted for orientation, but disbelieved or rejected for gender identity. Each challenge can layer onto our foundational attachment style, distorting or reinforcing it.

Connecting old lessons to present bonds

If you've ever felt compelled to send repeated texts or calls, terrified your partner's silence signaled abandonment, or if you've shutdown emotionally the moment your boyfriend asked for deeper closeness, you've encountered the reflexes shaped in earlier years. Attachment theory gives us the vocabulary to label these reflexes and the tools to transform them. Rather than dismissing ourselves as "broken" or "too needy," we can say: "Ah, that's my anxious side," or "This is my dismissive habit," or "I see the push-pull of my fearful approach." With awareness, we reclaim choice over habits that once felt automatic.

Understanding attachment theory: a gay-centric overview

John Bowlby's secure base

John Bowlby, often called the father of attachment theory, observed that children explore the world more confidently if they know a caregiver stands ready to comfort or protect them—like a stable base within the woods from which you can roam freely (Bowlby 1979). If that base is shaky, you might feel clingy or avoid exploring. For gay men, this "shakiness" can be amplified by family discomfort around orientation or gender expression. You might have had parents who were warm in general but uneasy when you displayed so-called "feminine" traits, or you might have faced outright hostility. Those mixed or negative signals from childhood can shape your entire approach to closeness.

Mary Ainsworth's strange situation

Mary Ainsworth tested children's reactions when a caregiver left them briefly and then returned (Salter Ainsworth *et al.* 1978). She spotted four common response patterns:

- *Secure:* The child shows mild distress at separation, but re-engages happily upon reunion.
- *Anxious-preoccupied:* The child becomes extremely upset, clinging even after the caregiver returns.
- *Dismissive-avoidant:* The child appears unbothered by the departure and avoids the caregiver upon return.
- *Fearful-avoidant (disorganized):* The child exhibits contradictory, often confused responses—wanting closeness yet seeming scared or disoriented.

As these children grow into adults, they typically replicate similar behaviors in relationships. If you felt your orientation or identity wasn't acceptable, you might show an anxious-preoccupied style (constantly hoping to prove you're worth staying for) or a dismissive-avoidant style (putting up walls to avoid more hurt). Or you could flip between the two—fearful-avoidant—longing for affection one moment and panicking the next.

Why attachment is key for gay men

Because gay men often experience added rejection or conditional acceptance, our early attachment scripts might be overshadowed by secrecy, shame, or partial support. Maybe a father said, "I love you," but also insisted you "Act normal around relatives." Or a mother might have simultaneously coddled and condemned you, fueling confusion. Attachment theory helps us see how all this merges into distinct patterns that can appear in adult love, work relationships, or close friendships.

The four main attachment styles

Here's a quick overview before we dig into the specifics:

- Secure:
    - Balanced, comfortable with emotional expression and independence.
    - Trusts that conflicts won't ruin the bond.
- Anxious-preoccupied:
    - Yearns for closeness, fears abandonment, can appear clingy or overly "needy."
    - Sees potential rejection in small shifts, needing constant reassurance.

- Dismissive-avoidant:
  - Prefers autonomy, minimizes need for emotional depth.
  - May treat intimacy as burdensome or a threat to independence.
- Fearful-avoidant (disorganized):
  - Push-pull dynamic, craving closeness yet fleeing if it gets too real.
  - Often linked to chaotic or traumatic childhood experiences.

In what follows we'll explore each style in detail, describing typical childhoods that set the stage, how it might show up for gay men, and ways to adapt or heal as an adult.

Style #1: secure attachment

Definition

Secure men approach relationships with a basic trust in closeness. Conflicts can arise, but they don't assume it signals the end. They're comfortable offering and receiving support, and they don't feel threatened by their partner's independence. They can say "I'm upset" calmly, expecting understanding rather than catastrophe.

Typical childhood roots

A secure style often emerges when at least one caregiver was reliably warm and available. Even if your orientation wasn't fully understood, you may not have faced overt rejection. For instance, a mother might have said, "I don't quite get it, but I love you anyway," or a father might have quietly accepted that you were different without constant ridicule. This steadiness teaches you that love can be consistent and safe.

SECURE ATTACHMENT
Idris and Kenji

Idris (mid-thirties, cis gay man, teacher) grew up in a family where minor quirks were celebrated; though no one explicitly championed his gay identity, he also wasn't chastised for it. When he came out in high school, it wasn't a shock. As a result, Idris rarely doubts he's lovable.

With Kenji (thirties, cis gay man, data analyst), Idris freely asks for help if a batch of grading overwhelms him, trusting Kenji to empathize without judgment. Kenji feels equally free to discuss career anxieties, believing Idris won't brush him off. The relationship weathered a few rocky points (like tension over how "out" to be at family gatherings), but each time they tackled it through open dialogue.

How this style handles everyday life

- *Family pressures:* Homophobic relatives might still test your resilience, but you're likely to talk it through with your partner or chosen family, not hide it.
- *Minority stress:* If your boss cracks a homophobic joke, you might share the hurt and problem-solve together with your partner, believing empathy awaits at home.

Practical tips

- *Maintain openness:* Keep naming external stressors so they don't accumulate silently.
- *Celebrate small acts:* Note each time you and your partner handle disagreements calmly. These mini-successes keep the relationship resilient.
- *Beware erosion:* Even secure men can slip into insecurity under chronic prejudice or unresolved trauma. Regularly check in with your partner about small concerns.

Style #2: anxious-preoccupied attachment

Definition

Anxious men crave intimacy yet fear it might evaporate. They can interpret small signs—like a partner's delayed reply—as a signal of disinterest or impending breakup. Conflict triggers worry about being abandoned, leading to "clingy" or controlling behaviors, though the underlying emotion is panic.

Typical childhood roots

This style often arises if caregivers were inconsistent: sometimes warm, sometimes dismissive. Imagine a mother who was affectionate but occasionally made comments like, "Stop being so dramatic—it's embarrassing." Or a father who offered approval only if you matched certain expectations of masculinity. This fluctuation teaches you that love is conditional and can vanish if you misstep. As a child, you might have learned to watch for the slightest sign of disapproval, fueling hypervigilance.

ANXIOUS-PREOCCUPIED ATTACHMENT

Zayd and Taro

Zayd (late twenties, cis gay man, freelance designer) was praised when he did "masculine" things but occasionally shamed for anything seen as effeminate. He grew up hearing "We love you, but don't act too gay." That conditional acceptance lingers, so in adulthood, he clings to Taro (thirties, cis gay man, researcher), terrified that any moment Taro might leave.

If Taro's texts slow down, Zayd's anxiety roars: "He's bored with me." Therapy helps him realize these are old triggers, not actual signals of rejection. They set a calm check-in each night so Zayd feels steady without Taro feeling smothered.

How this style handles everyday life

- *Body image fears:* If gay culture emphasizes a certain look, you might fixate on perceived flaws, believing any imperfection dooms you to be dumped.
- *Dating apps:* The endless array of options can reinforce, "You're replaceable."
- *Coming-out trauma:* Rejection from family might linger, making each new conflict a potential reenactment of abandonment.

Practical tips

- *Pause before reacting:* If you sense panic at a slow text, set a timer for 10 minutes before sending a follow-up. This buffer can calm immediate anxiety.

- *Self-soothing techniques:* Try breathing exercises, guided meditations, or short affirmations like "A delay doesn't equal rejection."
- *Communicate clearly:* Voice your needs to partners without attacking: "I'm feeling anxious when I don't hear from you all day. Can we arrange a quick midday check-in?"

Style #3: dismissive-avoidant attachment

Definition

Dismissive men emphasize independence, often seeing emotional depth as a nuisance. They might avoid discussing conflicts or deeper feelings, brush off compliments, or label concerns "overreactions." Underneath lies a learned belief: closeness equals risk, so it's safer to remain self-reliant.

Typical childhood roots

Dismissive patterns form if a child's emotions were neglected or belittled. If you expressed fear or sadness and a parent said, "Stop whining," you learned to keep vulnerabilities hidden. If your "difference" (being gay or trans) was either ignored or mocked, you might double down on independence, concluding that people can't be trusted to handle your true self kindly.

DISMISSIVE-AVOIDANT ATTACHMENT
Anil and Stefan

Anil (thirties, cis gay man, finance manager) recalls a father who ridiculed his "feminine" traits while his mother rarely offered emotional support. He grew up thinking, *Show no weakness*. As an adult, if Stefan (thirties, cis gay man, artist) tries to discuss emotional closeness or their future, Anil dismisses it as unimportant, leaving Stefan feeling pushed away. Over months, Anil notices how this pattern starves genuine intimacy. Through small steps—like saying, "I felt stressed at work today"—he learns that sharing vulnerability doesn't always lead to mockery.

How this style handles everyday life

- *Public affection:* You might resist holding hands, claiming, "I'm just not into PDA [public displays of affection]," but the deeper reason might be fear of exposure or judgment.
- *Conflict strategy:* You might go silent, avoid or trivialize the issue, and revert to "I'll handle it myself."
- *Partner reactions:* Your partner can feel neglected, leading to repeated conflicts about "Why won't you let me in?"

Practical tips

- *Share one small feeling daily:* Even naming mild annoyance at a coworker can break the habit of total emotional silence.

- *Clarify intent:* If you need space, say, "I need a moment to process—I'm not dismissing you." This helps your partner understand you're not rejecting them personally.
- *Reflect on old messages:* Journal about childhood statements that taught you to hide your feelings, and gently question if they still serve you.

Style #4: fearful-avoidant (disorganized) attachment

Definition

Fearful-avoidant men simultaneously crave closeness and believe it's dangerous. They might be highly affectionate for a week, then vanish or sabotage the relationship.

Typical childhood roots

A child who sees a caregiver vacillate between nurturing and punishing, or experiences sudden betrayals, can grow into an adult who's never sure if intimacy will be safe or catastrophic. For a gay or trans child, extreme mixed signals might show up: a sibling who is supportive but a parent who condemns you, so you internalize the idea that "people might turn on me at any second." This style usually develops when a child experiences inconsistent or traumatic caregiving—love that arrives one day, and hurt the next, teaching them that connection can rapidly turn threatening.

FEARFUL-AVOIDANT ATTACHMENT

Dev and Alain

Dev (late twenties, cis gay man, marketing) occasionally dreams aloud about a shared future, but if Alain (thirties, cis gay man, personal trainer) responds enthusiastically, Dev suddenly withdraws, citing "I need space." In childhood, Dev's father was sometimes kind, sometimes raging if Dev seemed "too soft." Now Dev's reflex is to run the moment closeness feels real. Therapy helps him label the underlying panic so he can pause and say, "I'm triggered," instead of shutting Alain out for days.

How this style handles everyday life

- *Unpredictable behavior:* Cancelling plans last minute if you sense your partner is "too eager."
- *Lingering trauma:* Possibly from bullying, assault, or forced secrecy. You might both want community and avoid it, leading to inconsistent involvement in gay social circles.
- *Partner's reaction:* Your partner may feel emotionally whiplashed, uncertain how to respond when you abruptly vanish after an intimate evening.

Practical tips

- *Build micro-routines:* Simple daily check-ins or rituals can provide a sense of safety and predictability.

- *Name the panic:* Instead of disappearing, say, "I'm feeling overwhelmed—can we take a break and revisit this in an hour?"
- *Professional help:* Fearful-avoidant patterns often tie to deeper trauma. An LGBTQ+-affirming therapist or support group can help unravel old wounds.

Typical childhoods for each style

While we've woven childhood snapshots into each style, let's condense them here:

- Secure childhood:
  - *Atmosphere:* Warm, reliable care. Even if not explicitly pro-gay, caregivers generally showed acceptance of the child's unique traits.
  - *Result:* The child learns to trust closeness, handles conflicts calmly, and believes relationships are stable.
- Anxious-preoccupied childhood:
  - *Atmosphere:* Inconsistent affection—sometimes nurtured, sometimes criticized. Any "non-masculine" behaviors might trigger disapproval.
  - *Result:* The child grows uncertain about their lovability; they become hyper-alert to signs of rejection, often overanalyzing small shifts.
- Dismissive-avoidant childhood:
  - *Atmosphere:* Caregivers neglect or belittle emotions.

Possibly strict rules on masculinity, ignoring or mocking "softness."

- *Result:* The child learns to be self-reliant, viewing vulnerability as a liability. Hiding any "feminine" or gay-leaning traits becomes a norm for self-preservation.

- Fearful-avoidant (disorganized) childhood:
  - *Atmosphere:* Unpredictable or traumatic parenting, sometimes supportive but also punishing. Could be serious conflict, abuse, or contradictory acceptance.
  - *Result:* The child associates love with danger, leading to approach-avoid cycles in adulthood.

Intersectional factors: layering complexity

Cultural norms, race, and faith

Attachment doesn't blossom in a vacuum. If you're a person of color in a predominantly white gay scene, you might face racism plus homophobia, deepening anxious or dismissive tendencies. If you're from a religious family that sees "acting gay" as sinful, you could become fearful, never sure if a moment of acceptance might flip into condemnation. Each identity—Black, Latino, Asian, Deaf, older adult, trans—carries unique experiences, shaping how you respond to closeness.

Societal pressures

- *Older age:* Surviving earlier eras of rampant homophobia

or the AIDS crisis might have fostered a dismissive stance: "I learned not to trust easily."

- *Trans identity:* If your family accepted your orientation but rejected your gender identity, you might develop a fearful-avoidant style from the contradictory messages.
- *Disability:* Navigating gay spaces that aren't accessible or where you're fetishized can amplify feelings of either anxious desperation for acceptance or dismissive "I don't need you anyway."

Recognizing these overlapping paths is vital. If you see your childhood might have yielded a secure base but then repeated hostility in adolescence triggered anxious behaviors, or if your once manageable anxious style worsened after a traumatic breakup, you're validating the complexity of your forest environment.

A personal reflection

I was in my early twenties when it dawned on me how tightly I kept my guard up. My grandmother insisted, "It's just a phase," or "You won't go to heaven like this," and casual slurs from peers reinforced that closeness meant risk. I took a dismissive route, telling myself I didn't need love. Yet, by my mid-twenties, I noticed a craving for real connection. If someone tried to show affection publicly, I'd feel a rush of fear and longing in equal measure. Reflecting now, I see the seeds of a more *fearful-avoidant* pattern: at one moment, I'd long for acceptance, and the next, I'd vanish, terrified of betrayal.

Unraveling that script took patience—journaling, therapy, practicing small moments of vulnerability. When I recognized my environment had carved that path, it freed me to build a new route. I discovered that each empathetic conversation or gentle embrace could reshape my assumptions about love. Some days I still freeze or want to run, but I'm slowly realizing that this forest is larger than I ever knew—and it contains more safe clearings than those old survival strategies allowed me to see.

Exercises to deepen self-awareness and adaptation

DISCOVER YOUR ATTACHMENT STYLE

Set the scene: Dedicate 15 minutes in a quiet spot—perhaps when you wake up or before bed.

Reflect on your childhood: Jot down any memories of seeking comfort or expressing your orientation. Was it met with love, fear, dismissal, or hostility?

Identify adult patterns: Think about romantic or close friendships. Do you chase reassurance? Do you rarely open up? Do you feel a push-pull?

Notice your bodily responses: Do you tense up at the slightest hint of conflict or feel instantly alone if a partner is delayed? That might be anxious-preoccupied. If you shrug off deeper talks, that might be dismissive-avoidant.

Choose one step: For example, if anxious-preoccupied, pause before rapid-fire texting. If dismissive-avoidant, offer one personal feeling daily. If fearful-avoidant, label the panic: "I'm triggered; I need a moment."

MAPPING YOUR RELATIONSHIP HISTORY

Draw a timeline: From early childhood to now, place key relational events on your timeline—first crushes, big breakups, acceptance or rejection episodes.

Mark the highs and lows: Were there moments a family member stood up for you? Times you felt heartbreak or betrayal?

Observe any patterns: For example, repeated cycles of you leaving first, or getting anxious after a few months, or being the caretaker who's "always there."

Connect to attachment: Do these experiences align with anxious-preoccupied, dismissive-avoidant, fearful-avoidant, or secure behaviors?

Reflect: Summarize your biggest insight in a journal: "I see that each time someone got too close, I found reasons to cut it off." Awareness sets the stage for new choices.

BUILDING HEALTHIER ATTACHMENT PATTERNS

Pinpoint your top three triggers: For example, your partner praising someone's looks, delayed responses, and them wanting more emotional depth.

Set a goal: If anxious-preoccupied, practice self-talk like *I am still lovable when I'm not actively performing*. If dismissive-avoidant, commit to one daily *I feel* statement. If fearful-avoidant, announce "I need a break but I'm not leaving you" rather than ghosting.

Adopt mindful strategies: Try meditation, short walks when panic arises, or calling a trusted friend for perspective.

Log mini-wins: When you manage a conflict without a meltdown or vanishing, note it. Celebrating these will help you believe in change.

A WEEKLY "CHECK-IN RITUAL"

For partners: Designate 20 minutes each Sunday to ask, "How are we doing? Anything we've been avoiding?" End with gratitude or a positive note.

If you are single: Use the same approach for personal reflection—"When did I feel secure or anxious this week? Did I approach it differently?"

Moving forward: how attachment shapes future chapters in this book

Attachment and conflict resolution

An anxious-preoccupied person may interpret a normal dispute as a sign their partner wants to leave, fueling panic. A dismissive-avoidant person might stonewall or shutdown, leaving the anxious partner frantic. Fearful-avoidant men might alternate between anxious meltdown and dismissive retreat. Recognizing these loops sets the stage for calmer communication techniques in upcoming chapters.

Attachment and intimacy

A dismissive-avoidant man might keep sex purely physical, avoiding emotional vulnerability; an anxious-preoccupied man might equate sex with proof of being wanted; a fearful-avoidant man might relish closeness one day and vanish the next. We'll explore how to move toward more mutually satisfying and stable intimacy in future chapters.

Attachment and self-worth

An insecure style can amplify shame from internalized homophobia or transphobia. A secure style can buffer against negative cultural messages. We'll look at how self-compassion—especially for those of you who grew up in invalidating environments—can gradually rewire our sense of worth.

Conclusion: mapping a path to healthier bonds

We've navigated a calmer clearing in the forest, illuminating how each attachment style—secure, anxious-preoccupied, dismissive-avoidant, and fearful-avoidant—interweaves with gay men's experiences of acceptance, rejection, and everything in between. You've seen how typical childhood contexts lay the groundwork for each style, and how external factors like racism, religion, or ableism can shape or intensify these patterns.

A final reflection

Which style resonates most with your typical behaviors? Perhaps you're anxious around new dates, or dismissive when conflicts arise, or mostly secure yet triggered by certain memories? A single insight—*I see where this came from*—can free you from feeling "broken." Each small step away from old reflexes (like calmly stating a need or pausing anxious urges) is a move toward rewriting your emotional map. This forest, once overshadowed by shame or fear, has open paths, if you know where to look—and each mindful choice can bring you to the next clearing of possibility.

A final self-check

What's one immediate change you can make this week? Pausing an anxious impulse? Offering a dismissive partner a gentle invitation to share? Or naming a fearful push-pull before it escalates? As you continue through the forest, remember you're not alone. The ground beneath your feet might be uneven, but with growing awareness and compassion, you forge the trails that lead to truer connection. Even if you stumble, each clearing offers a fresh perspective, proving again that closeness can be nurturing and safe, despite what old lessons or a biased world once taught you.

CHAPTER 4

Nurturing the Inner Self

Embracing Self-Compassion and Acceptance

We've already journeyed across challenging emotional ground—navigating personal traumas, societal judgment, and family narratives that can undermine our worth. Imagine, now, that we enter a calm, sunlit clearing in this metaphorical forest, stepping away from the thickets of external pressure to focus more gently on ourselves. In this chapter, we explore *self-compassion* and *self-acceptance*, two protective forces that can soften shame-based thoughts, heal the residues of rejection, and anchor us in a deeper sense of wholeness.

Why do these concepts matter so much for gay men, including trans gay men? We often grow up enduring microaggressions or overt hostility. Our identities might be questioned, our expressions misunderstood, and even those who try to love us sometimes fail to affirm our dignity wholeheartedly. Through self-compassion, we develop an internal ally—a nurturing voice that counters the negativity embedded in culture, religion, or family traditions. This chapter delves into why self-compassion is transformative, what the research says, how affirmations can be tailored for authenticity, and how to weave these practices into daily routines without turning them into empty slogans. We'll also address typical pitfalls—like inconsistency or ignoring deeper traumas—so you can adopt these techniques with realistic goals in mind.

A personal reflection

I recall a time, not so long ago, when I believed kindness was something I offered only to others. Whenever I stumbled—whether from a failed date, a relative's critical remark, or a day haunted by thoughts that my orientation was a liability—I'd unleash self-criticism as if punishing myself would fix all the "flaws" that seemed to bother everyone else. Instead of helping, it just locked me into a grim cycle of shame.

It was a therapist—himself a gay man—who finally helped me see how unforgiving I'd been toward myself. "You're so compassionate with other people's struggles," he noted one day, "yet you attack yourself for the same vulnerabilities." Something in me cracked open at that observation. I realized I'd poured empathy into everyone else's wounds while treating my own with cold indifference. From that point on, I decided to experiment: each time my mind veered into blame—*You're a failure, you'll never measure up*—I'd pause and wonder, *What if I offered myself the same kindness I'd give a dear friend?*

It was far from easy. Like learning a new language, the practice felt alien. Some days, I managed to replace a harsh critique—*You should be tougher*—with a gentle reminder: *It's understandable you're upset; you deserve support.* But there were also slips. Occasionally, I'd catch myself lapsing into the old script, berating myself for not "getting over" a problem faster or for failing to meet some imagined standard of masculinity. Each of those setbacks stung, yet I realized the shifts didn't vanish; they only wavered. Over time, the gentle approach began to take root, wearing down my self-reproach bit by bit.

No, it didn't fix everything overnight. But day by day, I noticed I was quicker to show compassion when I felt insecure, or when a harsh remark brought back old insecurities. And whenever I saw myself sliding into old habits, I'd remind myself: "Yes, this is hard—but it pays off. You're allowed to stumble and still be worthy of understanding." Eventually, I found a supportive internal voice growing stronger, ready to say: *It's okay to feel this way—you're only human*, reminding me that self-kindness, once so foreign, can indeed become second nature.

Why it matters: This personal anecdote highlights the dramatic difference self-compassion makes. Many of us, as gay or trans gay men, grew up in environments that questioned or ridiculed us. Learning to be gentle with our insecurities can break cycles that go back to childhood.

Up next, we'll discover why these shifts are so crucial in the broader picture of mental and emotional well-being.

Why self-compassion matters for gay men

Confronting internalized negativity

The roots of self-critique

Gay men—cis or trans—are often burdened by cultural expectations about how a "real man" should act. Whether from strict religious upbringing, casual homophobic remarks in school, or microaggressions in social spaces, we're taught, in subtle or blatant ways, that we're "not enough" or "off." Over time, these messages can harden into an inner voice that scolds or shames us, turning external condemnation into internal law.

Self-compassion as a direct antidote

Here's where self-compassion steps in as a counterforce. Researchers such as Kristin Neff and Christopher Germer (Neff and Germer 2018) have documented how responding to adversity with kindness rather than self-attack reduces stress and curbs destructive rumination. In simpler language: whenever you catch yourself reliving a humiliating memory or bracing for judgment from a stranger, you can intentionally shift to a friendlier tone—*This is painful, and I deserve empathy, not more harm.* Repeatedly doing this rewires your inner landscape, challenging the inevitability of self-critique. For gay men, each gentle response can peel away the embedded shame so many of us carry from adolescence onward.

Internalized negativity acts like a thick vine in our forest, strangling self-esteem. Self-compassion cuts those vines by reminding you that other people's prejudices don't reflect your inherent worth. Next, we'll examine how it helps heal the deeper wounds of rejection that can linger for years.

Healing shame from past rejections

Echoes of hostility

Many of us can point to a specific memory—a friend who turned on us, a relative who insisted our orientation was "just a phase," or a faith leader who equated our love with immorality. Such incidents often morph into stubborn shame triggers: random daily events can bring those moments rushing back, stirring guilt or self-hatred. If you're a trans gay man, add to that the possibility of being told you're not "really" the gender you claim, layering extra confusion and hurt.

Soothing those old hurts

Self-compassion invites you to reapproach these memories with understanding. Paul Gilbert's work (2014) in compassion-focused therapy suggests that meeting shame with warmth weakens the neural pathways that keep us stuck in negative loops. Practically, it means if your mind replays being called "disgusting" after coming out, you respond gently: *That was cruel, and I'm sorry you went through it. You aren't disgusting; you deserve respect.* The more consistently you do this, the less that memory defines your sense of self.

Why it matters: Think of it as an emotional "reparenting"—offering the kind, accepting words you might have craved back then. Over time, your relationship to that past event shifts: instead of a painful legacy that fosters shame, it becomes a recognized wound you're actively healing through self-kindness.

Now let's see how this compassionate stance impacts the way we connect with others, especially in friendships and relationships.

Strengthening community bonds

Less defensive, more empathetic

When you no longer see yourself as unworthy, you're less apt to lash out or retreat in interactions. If a loved one criticizes something you do, you're better able to step back and think, *That hurts, but maybe I can understand where they're coming from*, rather than launching into, *I knew I wasn't good enough—time to push them away*. In essence, self-compassion reduces the self-protective reflexes that sabotage closeness, making you calmer and more open in dialogue.

Modeling a healthier dynamic

Moreover, being gentle with yourself sets a precedent for how you treat others. In a group of gay men, for instance, if one friend admits struggling with body image, a self-compassionate person might say, "I get that. It's tough, but you're not alone," instead of issuing tough love or ignoring the emotional reality. This nurturing approach can ripple outward, fostering a broader culture where we support each other's vulnerabilities rather than ridiculing them.

Self-compassion not only dissolves internal shame but enriches external relationships by reducing defensive reactivity and promoting empathy. Next, let's dig into the research that helps us understand how these shifts happen on a psychological and even neurological level.

The science behind self-compassion

Halting negative cycles

Key studies on self-compassion

Kristin Neff's research (Neff and Germer 2018) indicates that self-compassion reliably correlates with lower anxiety, decreased depressive symptoms, and improved emotional resilience. Translated simply, it means that when you face adversity—like a stressful day at work or an old memory of being teased in high school—adopting a kind, rather than critical, internal voice helps you bounce back faster. Ashley Allen and Mark Leary (2010) similarly observed that people who practice self-compassion recover more steadily from perceived failures, resisting the urge to spiral into self-blame.

Implications for gay men

Since many of us endure repeated incidents of belittlement or invalidation, these scientific findings underscore how crucial it is to short-circuit negativity at its onset. If you've internalized the belief that you're "too effeminate," self-compassion counters that label each time it arises—*I'm allowed to be who I am, and my softness doesn't undermine my strength.* Over days, weeks, and months, the mind recalibrates, taking such statements seriously.

Research backs up the intuitive sense that kinder self-talk helps. Now we'll move into how to put these insights into practice, especially focusing on affirmations and structured daily habits.

Practical approaches

Shaping credible affirmations

Honesty over hyperbole

Declaring *I'm flawless* when you're feeling down can ring hollow. Instead, opt for statements like, *I'm doing my best, and it's okay not to be perfect.* That incremental shift is easier to believe, so your mind accepts it rather than dismissing it. Pairing it with a gentle physical gesture—like a hand on your chest—can anchor the message in your body. Neuroscience findings (Hölzel *et al.* 2011) imply that bodily reassurance quiets stress centers, reinforcing the affirming statement.

Regular repetition

Affirmations work best if they're woven into daily life rather than uttered randomly. Perhaps each morning, say, "I'm allowed to learn and grow today," before checking your phone. Or every evening, note one instance of self-compassion: *I didn't bash myself when I messed up that project*. The key is consistency—small acts repeated over time can transform the mental environment from punishing to nurturing.

Now that we know how to form affirmations that feel genuine, let's see them in action through real examples of gay men or trans gay men responding to challenges with this new, kinder perspective.

SELF-COMPASSION IN EVERYDAY LIFE

Javier and body image

Why this example? Body image issues plague many gay men, fueled by stereotypes that we must be lean, muscular, or perpetually groomed. Javier's story reveals how self-compassion counters these pressures.

Scenario

Javier (thirties, cis gay man) grew up equating success in gay spaces with having a perfect physique. Each morning, he'd poke and prod at perceived flaws, calling himself "lazy" for not working out hard enough. This routine left him anxious and ashamed by breakfast.

Self-compassion in action

Realizing the toll it was taking, Javier began pausing whenever negative thoughts flared. He'd mentally name the discomfort—*I'm feeling inadequate right now*—and offer a small reassurance: *My body deserves kindness, even if I have goals to improve it*. This approach didn't dissolve his body concerns overnight, but it softened the hateful tone he used on himself. Gradually, Javier discovered that gentler self-talk led to more balanced health habits. He still pursued fitness, but no longer punished himself mentally for not looking like an Instagram model.

Key lesson

A realistic affirmation—*I can care for my body without hating it*—proved far more healing than extremes such as *I'm the hottest man alive*, which rang false in the face of his insecurities.

Mariana, a trans gay man facing dating disclaimers

Why this example? Trans gay men confront both general homophobia and transphobia, and even gay-specific dating platforms can hold additional barriers.

Scenario

Mariana (twenties, trans gay man) frequently saw disclaimers like "No trans men" on profiles, a dagger to his sense of manhood. Initially, he internalized the rejection—*Maybe I'm just not man enough*.

Self-compassion in action

Through mindful reflection, Mariana started pausing whenever he felt that pang of shame. He'd take a slow breath, place a hand on his chest, and affirm, *I'm a valid man, regardless of who refuses to see it*. By acknowledging his hurt yet insisting on his own worth, Mariana found he could navigate apps or social spaces without internalizing every snub as personal failure.

Key lesson

A grounded affirmation—*My identity is real, and someone else's ignorance doesn't negate it*—helped Mariana decouple strangers' prejudice from his self-esteem.

Terrence's journey of self-compassion

Why this example? Terrence's story highlights how self-compassion intersects with racism in gay spaces and homophobia in Black spaces, illustrating how multiple biases compound.

Scenario

Terrence (thirties, Black cis gay man) loved socializing in clubs, but constant microaggressions—like men fetishizing him or ignoring him entirely—made him feel invisible. Simultaneously, certain relatives criticized his orientation, suggesting he was betraying his cultural roots.

Self-compassion in action

Torn between these opposing judgments, Terrence started journaling each night. He wrote, "I felt invisible at the bar tonight, and it stung." Then he applied a compassion-based response: "I deserve to exist without having to prove myself worthy of acceptance." Gradually, Terrence built an internal refuge, so each new slight felt less like a personal indictment. He sought out friend groups and events more inclusive of people of color, reinforcing his sense that he could be fully himself—a proud Black gay man—without apology.

Key lesson

Compassion isn't a naive shield ignoring racism or

homophobia, but it prevents those external biases from mutating into internal shame.

Overcoming common obstacles

Inconsistency in practice

The challenge

You read about self-compassion, try it once, and expect an instant shift. When negativity persists, you might assume you "can't do it" and give up.

The solution

Build a simple daily structure: perhaps a quick morning check-in—*How do I feel? Which affirmation can I try today?*—and an evening reflection—*Did I respond kindly when shame flared?* Over weeks, these micro-practices accumulate, rewiring your reflex from scorn to solace.

Bridging to the next obstacle: Beyond inconsistency, some fear self-compassion is just self-pity. Let's tackle that misconception next.

Confusing compassion with pity

The challenge

Men raised in tough, stoic cultures might conflate self-compassion with wallowing or weakness. They wonder if being gentle on themselves excuses poor choices.

The solution

Remember that real compassion includes accountability. For

instance, *I acknowledge I messed up at work, but I don't have to berate myself—I can correct the error and learn.* This perspective fosters growth rather than self-flagellation.

Bridging to the next obstacle: Self-compassion is about guiding yourself through mistakes, not denying them. Next, let's see how ignoring intersectional realities can derail an otherwise sincere practice.

Ignoring intersectional struggles

The challenge

Some try to "fix" internal negativity while pretending external discrimination isn't real. If your workplace is homophobic or your religious community condemns trans identities, self-compassion alone won't solve everything.

The solution

Yes, self-kindness can mitigate shame, but it should also inspire real-world steps—like seeking affirming networks or setting boundaries with critical family members. Affirming *I deserve respect* might prompt you to find a more inclusive job or challenge offensive remarks.

Bridging to the next obstacle: Ignoring external prejudice is risky, but so is overlooking severe internal trauma that a simple affirmation might not heal. Let's discuss that next.

Trauma overload

The challenge

Deep-rooted trauma from abuse, bullying, or conversion therapy can make affirmations feel superficial. If you're grappling with flashbacks or intense triggers, telling yourself *I am worthy* might barely scratch the surface.

The solution

Seek professional help—a trauma-informed therapist who understands LGBTQ+ contexts can guide you in integrating self-compassion into broader healing strategies. Affirmations become one tool among many, reinforcing safety but not replacing specialized care.

Self-compassion thrives when used consistently, realistically, and with awareness of bigger issues—trauma, oppression, or environment. Next, let's create a simple blueprint to practice compassion day-to-day.

A structured approach to self-compassion

Step 1: recognize the trigger

If you catch a wave of shame—maybe from an insulting comment or a fleeting memory—pause to label what's happening: *I feel embarrassed*, or *I sense panic*. Emotion-focused therapy suggests naming the feeling dulls its power (Johnson 2020).

Step 2: offer kindness internally

Speak to yourself as you'd speak to a dear friend: *I see you're hurt; I'm sorry you're going through this. You're not alone*. This reparenting approach mends old voids left by parents or communities that lacked genuine acceptance.

Step 3: affirm carefully

Pick a phrase that fits your reality: *I can be gentle with myself, even in pain.* Pair it with a gentle touch—placing your hand on your heart, for example. Research (e.g., Hölzel *et al.* 2011) shows that supportive physical gestures can soothe anxiety responses, letting the affirmation sink in deeper.

Step 4: translate to real-world action

Compassion's final step is doing something with it. If your living situation fosters daily insults, self-kindness may motivate you to find safer housing or set firm boundaries. Affirmations aren't about passivity; they're about fueling changes that honor your worth.

With this blueprint in mind, let's explore how to integrate these steps into the rhythms of everyday life—routine moments, relationship dynamics, and, if needed, professional support..

Weaving self-compassion into daily life

Micro-moments of kindness

Think of self-compassion as small seeds scattered throughout your day. In the morning, before your phone floods you with social media posts or news, take a breath: *How do I feel? Stressed, optimistic, neutral? Whichever it is, I can be kind to myself.* Midday, if negativity spikes—perhaps after an offhand comment by a coworker—pause for 10 seconds: *This stings; I can ease up on myself for feeling hurt.* In the evening, review one event where you succeeded in practicing compassion—like noticing your panic about a potential date and calmly reassuring yourself rather than spiraling.

Frequent mini-check-ins build muscle memory. Over time, you'll find it easier to default to a supportive stance rather than self-condemnation when faced with everyday stressors.

Self-compassion in relationships

Partnered approaches

If you have a partner, share your strategies for self-kindness with them. Perhaps each night, ask: "Did we each show ourselves compassion today?" This fosters mutual support, making it natural to say, "I snapped earlier because I felt insecure, but I'm working on being kinder to myself." Hearing each other's progress reduces misunderstandings and builds empathy.

Chosen family and friend circles

Not everyone's biological relatives are loving or affirming. In that case, your chosen family or friend group can act as your main emotional fortress. Arrange a monthly "compassion circle" where you each confess a recent struggle and respond with encouraging words—like "It's okay you felt that; you're not alone." This collective exercise normalizes vulnerability, reminding you that gentleness is a group value.

Beyond personal or relational contexts, therapy or group work can deepen these practices if you crave more structure, especially if you face layered oppressions or trauma.

Therapy and group support

Professional guidance

Counselors versed in compassion-focused therapy (CFT) or mindful self-compassion (MSC) can help you systematically integrate affirmations and self-soothing techniques. They may add intersectional awareness—like addressing how racism or transphobia shapes your negative loops—so your practice is tailored to your reality.

Group spaces

Group therapy or support circles (often found in LGBTQ+ centers) let you witness others' journeys. Hearing how another gay man overcame internalized homophobia can echo your story, strengthening your conviction that self-compassion is possible, not just a passing trend. If your location lacks in-person options, moderated online forums can fill the gap, provided they cultivate respect for diverse identities.

Practical methods range from micro-habits to communal check-ins and professional therapy.

Now let's see how these principles adapt across different life stages—younger men, midlife, and older men—to show they're universally helpful.

Tailoring self-compassion by life stage

Younger men (teens/early twenties)

Common struggles

Many young gay men wrestle with intense identity questions—*Am I flamboyant? Am I masculine enough? Will I ever find love and acceptance?* If you're also trans, you might face doubly complicated concerns about your body or how the gay community perceives you. It's easy to conflate a single negative experience with an overall verdict on your worth.

Self-compassion's role

By adopting statements like, *I'm learning who I am, and each step is valid*, you normalize a fluid process of self-discovery. If a date or college friend reacts negatively, you remind yourself, *That stung, but it doesn't define me. I can feel hurt without turning it into a lifelong condemnation.* This realistic self-talk can keep you from burying your authentic self to appease fleeting social expectations.

Midlife men (thirties/forties)

Common struggles

Men in their thirties or forties may grapple with career stress, shifting friend groups, and possibly the challenge of balancing romantic or familial relationships. If you came out later, you might worry you're "behind" peers who grew comfortable in their orientation younger. Or, if you've been out for a while, you could face burnout from navigating microaggressions at work or social scenes.

Self-compassion's role

When that insecurity creeps in—*I should've had my life together by now*—a compassionate voice says, *My timeline is my own; I'm allowed to find stability at my pace.* That shift from regret or envy to acceptance disarms negative comparisons. If conflict arises in a relationship, acknowledging, "It's okay we disagree; I'm not unlovable because we argue," preserves your sense of self-worth rather than letting the disagreement spiral into self-blame.

Older men (50+)

Common struggles

Older gay men, particularly those who have lived through eras with harsher homophobia or the AIDS crisis, may carry deep scars—lost friendships, internalized guilt, or regrets about not coming out sooner. Some also struggle with feeling invisible in youth-centric gay spaces.

Self-compassion's role

This stage might call for affirmations like, *I survived immense trials, and my feelings of grief or longing are valid.* Grief-laden memories can be approached with kindness: *It's normal I mourn those I lost; I can hold sorrow and self-love at once.* Compassion helps you reconnect with both yourself and younger folks, sharing lessons about resilience and empathy that only come from lived experience.

Regardless of age, these examples confirm self-compassion fosters growth, whether you're forging new social ties or reconciling old grief. Let's wrap up by consolidating the chapter's main points and reaffirming how self-compassion transitions you from harsh self-talk to a gentler, more expansive acceptance.

From harsh self-talk to gentle acceptance

In this chapter, we paused in a luminous clearing of our emotional forest to explore *self-compassion* and *self-acceptance*—concepts that can radically shift how gay men, including trans gay men, relate to themselves. We saw how these practices counter internalized negativity, heal old wounds of rejection, and enable us to approach others with empathy instead of guardedness.

Here are some core insights:

- *Why it matters:* Growing up amid homophobia, transphobia, or familial disapproval often instills shame-based reflexes. Self-compassion disarms those reflexes by offering warmth in place of condemnation.

- *Backed by research:* Works by Neff, Germer, Allen, Leary, and others confirm that kinder self-talk lowers anxiety and fosters resilience. In everyday language, that means each gentle word to ourselves interrupts destructive loops.
- *Practical tools:* Affirmations must feel believable—such as *I'm allowed to learn from mistakes*—and can be paired with physical gestures like a hand on the chest. Consistency (e.g., morning reflections, evening recaps) cements these habits.
- *Common obstacles:* Avoid superficial positivity, ignoring real trauma, or expecting instant changes. Instead, see self-compassion as a skill requiring repetition and honest reflection.
- *Life stages:* Teens discovering their identity, midlifers juggling career or relationship shifts, and older men carrying deeper grief all benefit from self-kindness—though the specifics of what triggers shame will differ.

Conclusion

As you leave this chapter's calm clearing and return to the busier trails of life—work deadlines, family tensions, the swirl of dating apps—keep hold of one essential reminder: you can choose compassion each time you confront negativity, whether external or internal. When old insults replay in your mind, step back and think, *This was unfair—I can acknowledge it was hurtful without blaming myself.* Or when you feel uneasy about meeting new people, remind yourself, *I'm learning to accept my own pace, and that's enough for now.* These small, deliberate acts shift your emotional stance from tension to gentleness, helping you reclaim energy once spent on self-defeat.

Over time, you may notice that being kinder to yourself

changes more than your inner monologue: it transforms your friendships, your capacity for love, and even your approach to activism or community building. In a world that so often questions our right to exist freely as gay men—especially if we're trans—self-compassion becomes an unshakeable foundation. It doesn't shield us from every prejudice, but it ensures prejudice won't define our sense of self.

So take a breath, let your shoulders relax, and whisper something gentle: "I'm allowed to be me, flaws and all, and still deserve understanding." That is the essence of self-compassion. It might feel fragile at first, but with practice, it becomes a steady flame lighting your path, even in the darker corners of the forest. And in those moments of flickering uncertainty, you can remember: an empathetic, affirming voice dwells inside you, ready to offer solace and remind you that, no matter what, you are worthy of acceptance—both from yourself and from the world around you.

CHAPTER 5

Rebuilding Trust

Strengthening Relationship Foundations

We have traveled a winding path through our inner forests, uncovering how trauma, societal pressures, attachment styles, and self-compassion interact to shape our emotional lives. Now, we turn to *trust*—the underlying certainty that a partner, friend, or family member cares about our well-being and will remain emotionally present despite our vulnerabilities. Whether you're single and hoping to establish a trusting bond in the future, or already in a relationship seeking to mend or deepen intimacy, trust is the backbone of emotional security. It allows us to share fears, reveal insecurities, and navigate conflicts without descending into panic or suspicion. Yet for gay men, including trans gay men, trust can feel especially fragile if earlier acceptance was half-hearted, if our orientation or identity was shamed, or if repeated microaggressions taught us to keep our guard high.

This chapter explores how trust is built and broken, how old wounds can sabotage present relationships, and how step-by-step actions can reinvigorate a sense of safety. Along the way, we'll see that trust isn't binary—it grows or wanes depending on how consistently both sides respond with empathy and honesty. We'll consider the experiences of those in long-term intimate relationships, those dating or newly partnered, and those who are single, wanting to clarify their personal values around trust for future connections with partners, family, or friendships. By the chapter's end, you'll realize that trust, no matter how battered, can regenerate if nurtured through mindful practice.

A personal reflection

I once believed I'd found the man I'd grow old with—let's call him Mark. On the surface, everything sparkled: romantic getaways, thoughtful gifts, and sweet reassurances that made me believe maybe—just maybe—my deepest fears about love could finally be put to rest. But beneath that shimmer, subtler truths were brewing. We were both in intense phases of our lives—each pulled in different directions by career and ambition. We rarely paused to ask each other, "Are we okay? Are we still reaching for one another?"

I remember small things that started to gnaw at me—Mark always keeping his phone close, snapping if I asked simple questions about who he was talking to. When I tried to share my uneasiness, he'd flip the script, labeling me "needy" or "too sensitive." That hurt. And it also hit a nerve that's all too familiar for many of us gay men: the fear that expressing vulnerability will be met with shame or withdrawal. We often lack models for how to navigate closeness, so we learn to ignore the ache instead of naming it.

One weekend, my gut wouldn't quiet down. I looked through his messages. What I saw confirmed what I hadn't wanted to believe—explicit exchanges with another man, filled with plans and flirtation. I don't think affairs are ever just about sex; they're often about absence, disconnection, or buried wounds. But they're still a choice. And the deeper wound, I think, comes from avoiding real conversations, pretending it's not happening, or minimizing the harm done.

When I brought it up, I hoped for something—an apology, an explanation, anything real. But I got deflection, vague promises, and more silence. We tried couples therapy for a while, but it was clear we weren't in the same room, not really. I was doing the emotional heavy lifting, asking for honesty, for change, for repair. But change never came.

So I left. And yes, it was painful to lose him—but even more painful was losing my belief that love could be safe. That breakup didn't just end a relationship; it confirmed every old script I carried: that trust is foolish, that intimacy always ends in betrayal. Especially for gay men, where community can feel small and stakes feel high, it's easy to stay too long—hoping things will get better, even when they're slowly breaking you down.

But life surprised me. I met someone new—my current partner, who I've been with now for several years. And he did what Mark couldn't. When I said, "I feel scared—I need you to stay close," he didn't get defensive. He leaned in. He asked, "What would help?" And then he listened. No shaming, no eye-rolls, no calling me clingy. Just presence. Just care. And over time, that steady gentleness began to mend something in me I thought was broken for good.

Why it matters: This isn't a story meant to make Mark out as the villain. It's a story about how trust unravels when communication and accountability are missing. If you're unhappy, say something. If you're betrayed, know that you're not broken—just hurt. And hurt can heal. There *are* people out there who will treat your tenderness with care. Trust can be rebuilt, not because the past didn't matter, but because someone new chooses, again and again, to show you it does.

Why trust anchors relationships

Emotional safety: the core of closeness

Trust is essentially the confidence that someone will handle your insecurities and truths with care. For gay men and trans gay men, who may have spent adolescence or young adulthood hiding their orientation or identity, trusting someone means revealing a history of partial acceptance or outright condemnation. When trust flourishes, you can show your authentic self—quirks, fears, and all—and not expect ridicule or withdrawal. You talk about the pains of growing up closeted, or the confusion of navigating a hostile community, believing your partner or friend will respond with empathy rather than recoil. This emotional safety fosters real closeness, the kind that transcends superficial pleasantries.

Conflict resilience: working through, not running away

When trust is strong, conflicts no longer threaten to upend the relationship. You can argue about who handles the finances or how often you each need personal space, secure in the bond's capacity to weather tension. For many gay men shaped by negative experiences—like hearing "We love you but never mention that outside this house"—confrontations can feel dangerous. But if trust is stable, disagreements turn into problem-solving sessions rather than existential crises. You assume the relationship can survive mistakes, an assumption critical for personal growth. In this sense, trust acts like a safety net, letting you experiment with vulnerability without constantly fearing a devastating drop.

Shared growth: expanding together

Trust also sets the stage for *shared growth*. Without it, you might stifle your pursuits—like switching careers, or unveiling new sexual or emotional desires—because you fear your partner's rejection. Conversely, if you believe they'll remain supportive or at least open-minded, you explore new horizons with confidence. Over time, this synergy can deepen the relationship, forging not just a stable union but one that evolves and matures.

Trust is the quiet but firm scaffolding of emotional safety, conflict resilience, and personal expansion. For gay men and trans gay men who've experienced prior condemnation, trust is doubly important—yet also more vulnerable to wounding. Next, we'll examine how trauma, from seemingly small slights to overt abuse, can corrode the capacity to trust.

How trauma erodes trust

Trauma's many shapes and sizes

Trauma for LGBTQ+ individuals often isn't confined to one major event. It might be the constant microaggressions at school or from family, each one whispering, "You don't belong." Or it might be an intense, singular betrayal—like a violent assault or a religious authority pronouncing you an abomination. If you're trans, you might also face repeated refusals to honor your pronouns, or people insisting you're "confused," adding new layers of invalidation. Over time, each cut or assault forms a puzzle piece in a larger mosaic of distrust, teaching you that the world—and even close relationships—might be perilous.

The trigger-reaction spiral

When you have such a mosaic of wounded experience, minor triggers can spark disproportionate alarm. A partner who typically texts you promptly might, on a given day, be slow to respond. Instead of reading it as a normal variance, your mind leaps to suspicion—*He's with someone else; I knew it.* If your grandmother or father withdrew their support over your orientation, or if an ex-partner minimized your feelings, your baseline assumption might be that closeness always ends in treachery. This mental pattern is not irrational; it's how you learned to survive repeated dismissals or betrayals.

Recognizing old scripts

Acknowledging that your alarm bells might not reflect the current reality is the first step in addressing trust breakdowns. You become able to say, *I'm panicking, but am I reacting to my partner's actual behavior, or to echoes of my past?* By naming these old scripts, you short-circuit the automatic loop that leads to outsize conflict or withdrawal.

Now let's see how these complexities manifest in real-life contexts, from infidelity reconstruction to cultural challenges, from proactive disclosure of insecurities to single-life caution after betrayal.

Trust in action

To illustrate trust building or erosion in different relationship scenarios, let's delve into a few short stories, each capturing a unique dimension of forging and safeguarding trust.

REPAIRING INFIDELITY

Situation

Zane (thirties, cis gay man) and Niko (thirties, cis gay man) had been together for two years. When Zane, feeling unheeded, had an affair, Niko discovered it by chance—a friend saw Zane with someone else. Distraught, Niko confronted Zane, who ended the affair and vowed to rebuild their relationship.

Approach

They committed to weekly trust sessions, where Niko could voice anxieties while Zane provided consistent honesty about his daily life—no more unexplained absences. They saw a therapist who validated Niko's fury and delved into Zane's sense of emotional starvation. Initially, Niko believed Zane's remorse was superficial. Yet, over months, Zane's repeated displays of sincerity—like promptly sharing details of social outings or clarifying travel schedules—showed real willingness to repair.

Challenge

Moments of doubt flared: if Zane got home late, Niko's heart pounded with suspicion. But each time, Zane calmly explained, reaffirming the steps they'd practiced in therapy. Gradually, that cycle of mistrust softened, replaced by cautious acceptance.

Key lesson

Even major betrayals can be navigated if both parties commit wholeheartedly to consistent empathy and accountability. Compare this to my personal story with Mark, where repeated blame-shifting blocked meaningful repair, ultimately leading me to leave the relationship.

CULTURAL CLASHES

Situation

Kian (thirties, cis gay man) grew up in a conservative community that frowned upon direct confrontation, and lacked transparency around same-sex relationships. Axel (thirties, cis gay man) hailed from a liberal environment, convinced that immediate, direct talk was the best approach. Their long-distance romance was harmonious, but once together physically, they clashed over how to address tensions.

Approach

They arranged weekly emotional check-ins, letting Kian gently articulate his discomfort with blunt arguments. Axel realized Kian's "evasiveness" was culturally ingrained, not a personal slight. They adopted a pause rule: if friction rose, Kian could request a 20-minute break rather than escalate under pressure. Axel, though more direct, agreed to respect this breathing space.

Challenge

At one point, Axel broke the rule, insisting "We handle

this now!" Kian felt attacked, triggering old anxieties that direct confrontation threatened the entire bond. Seeing the negative impact, Axel apologized, reaffirming the compromise. Over time, each recognized that Kian's subtle approach and Axel's forthright style could coexist if they honored each other's comfort levels.

Key lesson

Cultural mismatches can breed mistrust if each partner interprets the other's style as dishonest or confrontational. Transparent communication about these roots—and small adjustments—can preserve and even deepen trust.

PROACTIVE INSECURITY DISCLOSURE

Situation

Ethan (thirties, cis gay man) wrestled with jealousy, while Sven (thirties, cis gay man) harbored a fear of being abandoned. Each had endured mild traumas with past partners—Ethan had been cheated on, Sven had been ghosted. Determined not to let these anxieties fester, they agreed on proactive openness.

Approach

They introduced the idea of naming insecurities by their third date, so no illusions built up. Ethan confessed, "I get jealous if you're chatting a lot with someone else," and Sven said, "I panic when I sense distance, because I've been ghosted." They also set daily check-ins—short calls or texts—preventing small concerns from snowballing. A playful approach eased tensions, using lines like, "Jealousy alert: code orange," to disarm the seriousness while still addressing it.

Challenge

Sven initially brushed off one of Ethan's jealousy concerns as "exaggerated." Realizing that stung deeper than he intended, Sven began validating Ethan's feelings instead. This consistent acceptance thawed Ethan's suspicions, enabling trust to bloom.

Key lesson

Early transparency about insecurities fosters a climate where trust can solidify.

Next, let's examine a scenario for those single and cautious after prior betrayals.

SINGLE AND POST-BETRAYAL

Situation

Evan (nineteen, cis gay man) had discovered a former partner was spinning elaborate lies about his job and finances, leaving Evan deeply shaken. After therapy, Evan decided to date again, but refused to rush trust.

Approach

Evan laid out boundaries on early dates: "I prefer gradual openness rather than jumping into exclusivity." Potential partners' reactions to this boundary revealed their respect level. Evan also tested empathy by disclosing a mild vulnerability around date three—like admitting he was once deceived about finances—to see if the new person responded with compassion or mockery.

No instant "perfect romance," but clarity. If someone trivialized his caution, Evan recognized a mismatch. Each time a date responded with kindness, Evan's trust in the possibility of healthy love slowly revived.

Key lesson

Carefully structured steps let single individuals re-engage with intimacy without ignoring their scars from past betrayals. If a date reacts poorly to minimal disclosures, it's a sign they may not be trustworthy for deeper emotional investment.

Exercises for strengthening or rebuilding trust

We've observed how trust fractures under betrayal, cultural friction, hidden insecurities, or personal history. Now let's integrate that knowledge into a set of structured techniques. These methods can aid those in relationships—repairing or strengthening trust—and those who are single—clarifying how they want to approach trust in future connections.

COMPOSING A TRUST TIMELINE

Goal: To create a visual record of major events shaping your trust stance—identifying patterns of betrayal or affirmation.

Find a calm hour to reflect. Draw a timeline from childhood

to present. Mark each event linked to trust formation: a grandmother's condemnation, a father's partial acceptance, a supportive friend who stood by you during a difficult coming-out, or a partner who cheated. For each, note how it impacted your sense of security. Did you lose faith in family? Did you develop an unspoken rule like, "Never rely on anyone completely"?

When you see mostly negative incidents, try to locate small pockets of warmth—a teacher who validated you, a cousin who surreptitiously offered acceptance. These spots indicate that trust can and does exist in your life, even if overshadowed by bigger heartbreaks.

Why it helps: By mapping your trust evolution, you notice how old injuries prime you to interpret current behaviors suspiciously. Recognizing that pattern is the first step toward reclaiming your present relationships from the grip of past misfortunes.

IDENTIFYING AND EMBODYING TRUST-BUILDING TRAITS

Goal: To define the personal qualities that underpin trust—honesty, empathy, reliability—and ensure you cultivate them consistently in your relationships or future encounters.

Reflect on what fosters trust for you. Write down five to seven core traits you consider essential—perhaps accountability, emotional availability, consistent follow-through, empathy, boundary respect, or transparency. Rate yourself on each trait from 1-10 (where 1 = not at all true of me and 10 = very true for me), acknowledging your strengths and weaknesses. If you see that you excel at empathy but struggle with emotional availability—often forgetting to respond or show up—commit to improving emotional availability over the next week. Log your daily or weekly progress.

If you're single, observe how you apply these traits in friendships or family contexts; if you're in a relationship, each partner could do this separately, and then compare notes. Strengthening these traits is a two-way proposition: as you become more trustworthy, you also model what you hope to see in others.

Why it helps: Often, we fixate on whether others can be trusted, ignoring our role. Trust thrives on mutual demonstration of key values. By living out these traits, you attract or reinforce connections with those who share them.

TRUST VISUALIZATION

Goal: To soothe anxious thoughts by rehearsing supportive, trusting interactions mentally, thus shifting from an automatic stance of fear to one of cautious openness.

Pick a quiet spot and close your eyes. Take a few deep breaths, releasing tension in your shoulders and jaw. Envision sharing a small but real concern—fear about finances, worry about health, or confusion about your gender expression—and imagine your partner, friend, or future companion responding kindly. Notice your body's shift from tension to relief. If skepticism intrudes—*That's impossible*—acknowledge it, then gently steer back to the supportive image.

After a few minutes, journal any insights or set a tangible next step, like *Tomorrow, I'll voice one mild concern to my best friend and see how he responds.* Repeating this visualization daily can gradually rewire your reflexive assumption that vulnerability leads to betrayal, replacing it with a measured hope that trust can be validated.

Why it helps: Our minds often default to worst-case scenarios, especially if prior traumas loom large. Visualization counters that negativity by building a new mental framework where supportive responses feel conceivable.

MICRO-EXPERIMENTS IN OPENNESS

Goal: To gather real-time evidence of whether someone is trustworthy through modest acts of disclosure or reassurance, while protecting yourself from oversharing too soon.

Select a slight vulnerability—*I've been anxious about a work project* or *I've felt a bit off about my body lately*—and share it with a person you'd like to trust more deeply. Pay attention to their reaction. Are they dismissive, or do they invite you to elaborate? If you see them belittling your feelings, you might limit future disclosures. If they respond with genuine warmth, you can gradually share deeper concerns.

Conversely, if you spot a friend or partner looking tense or worried, gently offer reassurance: "You seem uneasy; do you want to talk?" Notice how they react to your attempt at closeness. Keep a mental or written log of these mini-experiments. Over time, patterns will emerge:

certain people consistently show up with empathy, while others consistently dodge responsibility or shift blame.

Why it helps: Instead of leaping into blind trust or shutting everyone out, you methodically test each relationship's capacity for sincerity. This approach suits individuals who have endured repeated betrayals or microaggressions, as you proceed at a pace that respects your emotional boundaries.

Intersectionality and cultural nuances

Minority stress compounding distrust

For gay men or trans gay men navigating additional biases—racism, HIV stigma, ableism, older age discrimination, or a conservative faith tradition—trust can be undermined by repeated experiences of being reduced to a stereotype. That reality is well-documented in minority stress theory (Meyer 2003). If you carry multiple marginalized identities, you may question whether prospective partners or chosen family genuinely see you in your entirety, or only accept certain facets. This form of layered skepticism can damage trust early, preventing you from even attempting deeper connections.

Early clarifications

One protective tactic is to clarify important identity aspects or deal-breakers early on. If you live with HIV, mentioning U=U (Undetectable = Untransmittable) might reveal if a potential partner respects your health condition or treats it with ignorance. If you're trans, noticing whether someone bothers to learn your pronouns or how they respond to questions about your transition can forecast if trust can grow. If you experience racism in certain gay scenes, you may test a new friend's or partner's reaction to subtle boundary-setting, verifying their willingness to honor your comfort.

RACE, HIV, AND STIGMA

Malik (thirties, Black cis gay man with HIV) disliked how some men fetishized him for his race or reacted to his status with fear. Rather than wait for heartbreak, he gently asked potential dates about their views on race and HIV. Observing who responded with genuine curiosity and who dismissed his concerns allowed him to filter out those who might unwittingly reinforce destructive biases. Over time, he found that affirming connections could happen with those who recognized his full identity—race, HIV status, orientation—without belittling or "othering" him.

Why it matters: Trust can be doubly fragile if prior experiences taught you that people's acceptance might fade when confronted with your additional identity dimensions. But direct, incremental disclosures let you see if someone stands firm or buckles under prejudice. This method, combined with the exercises described, helps ensure you're building trust on a foundation that respects all parts of who you are.

Self-compassion tie-in: Building or rebuilding trust often triggers anxiety, especially if you've had experiences akin to discovering your fiancé was messaging other men behind your back. Every step, from sharing a mild insecurity to proposing couples therapy, can awaken old fears: *Am I setting myself up for betrayal again?* Recall from Chapter 4 how self-compassion can quell panic. A simple mental note—*I'm allowed to be scared, and I can still explore trust*—prevents reflexive self-sabotage. You might place a hand on your chest, breathing through the tension, and remind yourself that not every relationship will mirror your worst heartbreak. This gentleness ensures you remain open to verification—through micro-disclosures or direct questions—instead of letting trauma overshadow any chance of forging new security.

Attachment, accountability, and setting boundaries

Attachment and trust

John Bowlby's theory of attachment underscores how anxious, avoidant, or fearful tendencies can complicate trust. If you form an anxious-preoccupied style, you might constantly fear abandonment, reading harmless silence as a sign your partner is leaving. If you're dismissive-avoidant, you might resist closeness to dodge potential betrayal. Recognizing your style can help you adapt the trust exercises to your unique reflexes. For instance, an anxious-preoccupied person might find "micro-experiments in openness" extremely potent, learning to see that not every delayed reply signals doom.

Accountability in breaches of trust

When trust is broken, accountability is key to any chance of reconciliation. Harriet Lerner (2019) writes about the necessity of genuine apologies and transparent efforts to repair. Without accountability, no amount of longing or patience from the betrayed partner can resurrect trust. Think again of Mark in my personal reflection—he never truly owned his actions, constantly shifting blame onto my so-called insecurity, rendering meaningful reconstruction impossible. Conversely, if a partner or friend admits wrongdoing, expresses remorse, and consistently demonstrates changed behavior, trust can gradually sprout anew.

Setting boundaries around trust

Those who remain in a relationship post-betrayal might set boundaries to ensure forward progress. For instance, you might request regular check-ins if your partner once hid entire communications from you. If they refuse or perpetually forget, you see a mismatch between words and deeds. If you're single, you might define boundaries like "I won't become exclusive unless I see consistent follow-through for a couple months." Boundaries protect you from pouring trust into a dynamic that doesn't nurture it reciprocally.

Conclusion: the ongoing quest for trust

Trust in relationships isn't simply present or absent; it ebbs and flows based on the daily interplay of empathy, honesty, and reliability. For gay men and trans gay men who have confronted a history of half-baked acceptance or blatant hostility, trust can feel even more precarious. Yet each open conversation, each boundary set and respected, each instance of receiving or offering support invests a bit more security into the bond.

If both parties remain committed to these repeated acts of sincerity, trust can grow resilient despite earlier storms.

If you're single, consider these lessons as you approach future relationships—romantic or otherwise. Reflect on what trust means to you, and how to pace your disclosures or gather evidence of empathy before fully investing. If you are already partnered and facing trust fractures—be it from past trauma or a partner's current lapses—your next step might be the "trust timeline" or "micro-experiments," seeing if your partner is willing to match your efforts. Sometimes, if they continue to deflect or blame you (as Mark did in my story), the most self-affirming choice is to exit. Only you can gauge when trust's potential is exhausted, or if enough mutual accountability remains to salvage it.

A forward look

In the next chapter, we'll see how trust forms the bedrock for deeper emotional and physical intimacy—how you can lean into vulnerability without succumbing to panic. We'll also tie everyday rhythms—like conflict resolution styles and sexual communication—to sustaining trust in a real, ongoing sense. For now, reflect on which trust-building approach resonates with your life. If you're single, think about pacing your openness and looking for consistent empathy from future dates or new friends. If you're partnered, consider implementing a weekly trust talk or practicing micro-experiments in honesty. If fear spikes or old traumas resurface, recall your self-compassion anchor: you have the right to explore trust without being blamed for your caution.

Trust might feel elusive when past condemnations or betrayals loom large. Yet each small, consistent act—whether clarifying your feelings, setting boundaries, or verifying someone's empathy—cultivates new growth. Even in the face of heartbreak like the one I endured, trust can be restored in future relationships or new friendships, so long as accountability and genuine care are present. And if they're not? Recognizing that, and choosing to walk away, can be an equally valid step in preserving your own well-being and readiness for a bond that truly honors you.

CHAPTER 6

Deeper Connection

The Power of Intimacy and Vulnerability

In many personal narratives and cultural scripts, *intimacy* is painted as a finishing touch—an add-on we enjoy only after our careers, bodies, and mental health are all sorted. We often say, "I'll focus on real closeness once I've fixed every other piece of my life." Yet the more I observe others, guide clients, and reflect on my own experiences, the more I see that intimacy isn't a *bonus* or "dessert" at the end of our personal work; it's a dynamic element that sustains us throughout all of life's uncertainties.

For gay men—whether cis or trans—stepping into genuine emotional or physical closeness can feel precarious. We may have learned, through tense family dinners or casual slurs at school, that showing our soft underbelly is dangerous. By adulthood, that lesson lingers, making us wonder: *Will people still accept me if I reveal my hidden fears, my real desires, or the full truth of my body?* So, even when we crave deeper bonds, we might hold back.

In Chapter 5, we explored *trust*—the nourishing soil that allows a relationship (or even a profound friendship) to thrive. Now, we turn to *intimacy*—the seeds that sprout in that soil, blossoming into empathic communication, consistent tenderness, and shared vulnerability. Over time, these roots of closeness can anchor our relationships—or our sense of self if we're single—through life's fiercest storms.

Yet forging intimacy demands more than *just be vulnerable*. It also means *unlearning shame*—the burden from cultural or generational messages that depict same-sex love or trans identity as "less than," "too complicated," or "inherently deviant." Each shared laugh, each tearful admission of fear, helps rewrite these narratives. We'll also see how real-world influences—*chemsex, porn, internalized homophobia or transphobia*, and *intersectional realities* like race or HIV status—shape or hinder our capacity to connect. As you read, remember that trans gay men are integral to this conversation. Their experiences with readiness, body acceptance, and mainstream gay culture's assumptions may overlap with—and also differ from—those of cis gay men, enriching our collective insight into what deeper intimacy can look like in the entire gay community.

This chapter unfolds in the spirit of a continued trek through a dense emotional forest: earlier, we cleared brambles of trauma, built self-compassion, and fertilized the ground with trust. Now, intimacy invites us onto narrower paths where sunlight filters through. Each glimmer stands for a possibility of closeness, but old shadows remain. Fear or shame might still lurk, threatening to derail us. Yet, as we'll see, consistent empathy, honest self-reflection, and gentle self-kindness transform those pockets of fear into opportunities for genuine connection.

The shared trek toward openness: recalling the forest path imagery

Throughout this book, we've pictured our emotional lives as a vast forest. We've addressed traumas, recognized external pressures (like microaggressions, homophobic or transphobic slurs, or family condemnation), and learned how trust forms the emotional bedrock. Now, with *intimacy*, we step deeper into that forest. The sunlight filters through on narrow paths—revealing smaller clearings of potential closeness. However, the gloom of old insecurities might still lead to twists in our path. Intimacy can be thrilling and daunting in equal measure, especially for those of us who spent years guarding ourselves.

Thinking about intimacy and vulnerability, I recall a quiet evening, listening to a date share a memory of his mother's stinging remarks about his "effeminacy." My empathy flared because I recognized the same heartbreak from my own youth. In that moment, we both realized we'd been contorting ourselves to seem more "acceptable." A hush fell, and we each softened. It was a single exchange, but it carried us from superficial pleasantries to an honest, vulnerable domain. That's the subtle power of emotional intimacy: it unfolds not in grand declarations, but in these small moments where we *allow* the other to see our raw edges.

For gay men—cis or trans—this openness can counter decades of caution: "Don't act too feminine," "Don't mention you're trans," or "Don't share your real feelings." These protective strategies often arise because we're taught that revealing our true selves could invite ridicule or worse. Yet if we remain behind that fortress, we lose the richness of being truly known. Intimacy requires stepping out from behind curated personalities, letting ourselves be emotionally present—even if it means risking heartbreak. The payoff is profound: shared understanding, deeper trust, and the potential to rewrite old shame scripts with affirming experiences.

Why intimacy is profoundly healing: the antidote to shame and isolation

When we show someone a part of ourselves we typically hide—our self-consciousness about body hair or a scar from gender-affirming surgery—and they don't turn away, a piece of our old shame dissolves. Each acceptance rewrites that internal narrative, telling us, *Actually, you are worthy of love and empathy*. We touched on self-compassion in Chapter 4 and trust in Chapter 5—together, they lay the groundwork for intimacy to flourish.

> Consider Stephen (thirties, cis gay man), who once described himself as a "shameless flirt" but privately felt empty. Growing up in a conservative town, he believed revealing his true emotional self was forbidden. He masked his loneliness with confident banter and frequent hook-ups. Over time, these fleeting connections stopped satisfying him. In therapy, Stephen identified that real closeness felt scary–like a place he never had permission to occupy. The day he admitted, "I'm scared I'm too needy," he braced for me to confirm his fear. Instead, I welcomed his vulnerability, and he visibly relaxed. Through smaller steps–telling a friend he felt down, sharing a family trauma with a new date–Stephen learned that each tiny moment of openness invited closeness rather than scorn. This shift illustrates intimacy's healing effect: every empathic response disempowers shame.

For trans gay men, an added dimension might be the worry that their identity or body changes are "too complicated." The reassurance of a partner or friend who treats them as fully valid counters such worry directly. It affirms that being trans or having certain scars doesn't disqualify them from closeness.

We might recall the exact moment in childhood when a family member insisted our orientation was unnatural, or we recall a humiliating school incident. Intimacy invites us to bring that memory into the light, letting a caring person see it. When the other responds with compassion or understanding, it can rewrite the conclusion we once drew—*No one will ever accept me*—into a new reality: *Some people do accept me wholeheartedly.*

Trauma's echoes in closeness

Returning of past pains

Even if we've addressed many trauma triggers, closeness can unearth echoes we barely remember. Perhaps your partner's casual joke about your moaning triggers a memory of a past partner who mocked your vocal expressions. Or maybe a gentle stroke on your shoulder catapults you into recalling a nonconsensual experience from years ago. The body often retains these stories, surfacing them when we drop our guard. Recognizing this phenomenon can help us avoid self-blame; it's not that we're "broken" or "overly sensitive," but that our bodies are responding to old survival patterns.

Fight, flight, or freeze in intimacy

Imagine being on the verge of a passionate moment with a partner when a certain body position reminds you of a humiliating incident—maybe being teased by classmates or a relative's invasive comments. Instead of enjoying the present, you freeze. If you remain silent, your partner feels shut out.

By naming it—"Something about this position is bringing up a painful memory"—you reclaim control, opening space for your partner's empathy. Over time, these small disclosures can transform old triggers into shared understanding. Reinforcing that closeness doesn't have to be overshadowed by old trauma.

When two traumas collide

It's also common for both partners to carry scars. One might recoil when feeling physically confined because of past assaults, while the other might interpret that recoil as a sign of personal rejection. This feedback loop can spiral if unaddressed. Learning to say, "I'm panicking, but it's not about you—I need a breather" or "I sense you're uneasy; want to talk about what's coming up?" breaks the cycle. It turns potential conflict into an opportunity for deeper empathy.

Attachment styles revisited in the realm of intimacy

Four styles in the context of gay men

Earlier chapters introduced secure, anxious-preöccupied, dismissive-avoidant, and fearful-avoidant (disorganized) attachment. In intimacy—both emotional and sexual—these patterns become amplified, especially under stress. Let's briefly restate how they manifest:

- *Secure:* You handle closeness and independence smoothly, trusting that conflicts don't signal the end. You can talk openly about sexual preferences or emotional needs without meltdown.

- *Anxious-preoccupied:* You deeply desire closeness yet worry it'll vanish. You might over-please a partner sexually, always searching for reassurance: "Do you still want me?" or "Am I performing well enough?"
- *Dismissive-avoidant:* You might enjoy sexual acts but keep emotional distance. Physical desire may be fine, yet discussing insecurities or deeper feelings feels too invasive, threatening independence.
- *Fearful-avoidant (disorganized):* You crave love but repeatedly sabotage it, sometimes being affectionate, then abruptly pulling away. You might carry unresolved trauma that frames intimacy as both seductive and terrifying.

Intersectional nuance: A trans gay man with a fearful-avoidant style might have learned from repeated transphobia that closeness leads to invalidation, so he preemptively shuts down. A cis gay man of color with anxious-preoccupied tendencies might have endured racism in the dating scene, intensifying his fear that a partner will eventually leave. Recognizing these layers fosters compassion for ourselves and others. We're not "just anxious or avoidant," but shaped by multiple factors, from childhood rejections to adult microaggressions.

Emotional intimacy: sharing our inner worlds and going past surface talk

Emotional intimacy arises when we dare to move beyond daily facts—like, "I had a meeting at 10 am"—and reveal how we felt—perhaps the meeting left us uneasy, or a coworker's sly comment stung more than we expected. For gay men used to self-censoring, these admissions can feel monumental. Yet each time we let a friend or partner see that inner dimension, we deepen the bond.

HUMOR AND VULNERABILITY

Mark (thirties, cis gay man) has been seeing Jason (twenties, cis gay man) for a few weeks. Over dinner, Mark blurts out, "I worry you'll get bored with me." Jason, in turn, shares his own anxiety: "Sometimes I feel I'm too naive for you." Their shared laugh breaks the tension. Instead of posturing as "cool," they both show vulnerability, forging closeness. If you're single, practicing emotional depth with trusted friends can cultivate the skill for future romantic encounters.

Physical intimacy: from performance to connection

Reimagining touch as dialogue

Physical intimacy, especially in gay male culture, can be overshadowed by an emphasis on hooking up, sexual conquests, or rigid "role" identities (top/bottom/versatile/side). While none of these are inherently negative, focusing solely on *performance* can overshadow emotional presence. Intimacy is best seen as a conversation between bodies—where each movement or gesture expresses needs, desires, or vulnerabilities.

Body dysmorphia, gender dysphoria, and the fight against idealization

Many gay men wrestle with body image, seeing themselves as "too skinny," "not muscular enough," or "too old." For trans men, there may be concerns around scars from top or bottom surgeries, prosthetics, tucking, or binding. If we stifle these worries, sex can become fraught with tension—fearful we'll be "exposed" or found lacking. Openly naming them—"I feel insecure about my belly," "My chest scars might look shocking"—lets a partner respond supportively. Over time, compassionate acceptance reframes these perceived "flaws" into integrated parts of our shared experience.

Chemsex and porn influences: confronting the quick high and its impact on gay men

Chemsex—often involving substances such as crystal meth, GHB, or ketamine—promises a surge of libido and a fleeting feeling of invincibility, while porn offers instant arousal at the click of a button. At first glance, these may seem like harmless, even exciting, escapes from the weight of homophobia, transphobia, or everyday stressors. Yet for many gay men, including trans gay men, these quick fixes can unintentionally supplant deeper, more meaningful forms of connection.

Surveys and systematic reviews conducted across major urban centers have found that roughly one in five gay men report engaging in chemsex at least once, drawn by the allure of heightened pleasure or curiosity (Bourne *et al.*, 2015; Downing *et al.*, 2014; Tomkins *et al.*, 2019; Sewell *et al.*, 2018; Stuart, 2019). Another study indicated that a large proportion of gay men regularly watch porn, with over 70 percent admitting they rely on it as their primary outlet for sexual gratification. While neither chemsex nor porn is inherently "bad," consistent reliance on them can interfere with a person's capacity for real intimacy—numbing emotional nuance and undermining authenticity.

Eroding emotional depth through chemical highs

When chemsex forms the backbone of someone's sexual encounters, the act can shift from a potentially tender experience to a substance-fueled rush. Research from harm-reduction organizations like the Terrence Higgins Trust (2021) suggests that chemsex is frequently used by gay men to cope with deeper insecurities—ranging from body image worries to anxieties about masculinity or internalized homophobia. Under the influence, the mind is temporarily freed from shame, but the underlying issues remain unaddressed. As the high fades, many return to a baseline of isolation and guilt, sometimes amplifying preexisting mental health struggles like depression or anxiety.

Neurobiological studies show that dopamine spikes from stimulant use artificially inflate feelings of confidence and arousal, which can sabotage someone's ability to interpret a partner's emotional cues or communicate genuine needs (Berridge and Robinson 2016; Koob and Volkow 2016; Volkow *et al.* 2011). The result is often a cycle of chase and crash: an exhilarating chemsex session followed by a painful crash that leaves a deeper void, especially for those prone to self-criticism or who have faced repeated societal rejections.

Porn's unrealistic scripts and its consequences

Porn, while a widespread cultural touchstone, can also undermine intimate bonds if it becomes the primary template for sexual expectations. Surveys indicate that a high proportion of gay men feel pressured to conform to the "perfect porn body," fueling body dysmorphia and dissatisfaction (Duggan & McCreary, 2004; Brennan *et al.*, 2017; Filice *et al.*, 2020). The hyper-edited visuals and meticulously staged acts in porn rarely mirror the small, subtle signals that make real sex meaningful—nuances like eye contact that convey tenderness, or a reassuring squeeze of the hand that defuses insecurity. Repeated exposure to porn's exaggerated performances can warp someone's perception of what normal arousal, stamina, or even genitals "should" look like. This is especially devastating for trans gay men who may already be grappling with bodily dysphoria, as porn rarely depicts bodies that resemble their own. Studies on pornography's psychological impact reveal a link between frequent viewing and diminished satisfaction with actual partners, highlighting the risk that real-life closeness becomes overshadowed by fantasy-driven scenarios (Willoughby, Carroll, & Busby, 2016; Wright, Tokunaga, & Kraus, 2016; Stewart-Williams & Thomas, 2013).

Emotional numbing and self-sabotage

Both chemsex and porn, in their extremes, risk disconnecting gay men from authentic self-awareness. High or enthralled by explicit content, a person might gloss over a partner's subtle signs of discomfort or ignore personal boundaries. Over weeks or months, this pattern can spawn cycles of self-sabotage: chasing fleeting highs that sideline mutual empathy, only to wake up feeling hollow or remorseful. Behavioral psychologists note that shame can then intensify, fueling further substance use or bingeing on porn to escape negative self-talk. For gay men who already battle residual stigma about their orientation or identity, layering shame from sexual habits can solidify a narrative of unworthiness.

The social fallout

Beyond personal distress, chemsex and porn reliance can fragment broader social and romantic networks. Chemsex culture sometimes yields micro-communities centered purely on partying and hooking up, leaving those seeking emotional sustenance feeling alienated if they aren't also using. Friends or partners who voice concern may be dismissed as "uptight," while the individual in question becomes more isolated from the genuine closeness they actually crave. Persistent porn usage can create a hidden sense of inadequacy in relationships if one partner keeps comparing real intimacy to staged fantasies. Studies on relationship satisfaction among porn users underscore how unspoken resentments—like feeling overshadowed by an unrealistic standard—can fray bonds over time (Perry, 2017; Maddox, Rhoades, & Markman, 2011; Willoughby, Carroll, & Busby, 2016).

How to overcome the quick-fix trap:

- *Acknowledge the pattern:* The first step is recognizing when chemsex or porn ceases to be an occasional indulgence and becomes a default escape from underlying insecurities. Journaling or speaking with a trusted friend can help illuminate patterns—such as always turning to substances or explicit videos after a stressful day or an interpersonal conflict.
- *Seek specialized support:* For many gay men, healing necessitates resources tailored to LGBTQ+ experiences, like therapy or 12-step programs that grasp the cultural context of chemsex. Medical professionals and support groups can address the physical risks (e.g., overdose or STIs (sexually transmitted infections)) as well as the emotional ramifications. Couples therapy or open conversations about boundaries around porn can also quell misunderstandings and foster a sense of collaboration in dealing with these habits.
- *Relearn authentic intimacy:* Gradual reduction in chemsex or porn use can allow the rediscovery of authentic desire and

the subtle signals that build real-life erotic and emotional bonds. Sensate focus exercises and mindful sexual practices can help men reconnect with their bodies and those of their partners. Instead of chasing dramatic highs, they can explore a present, shared experience that values warmth and reciprocity over quick thrills.

- *Build a supportive network:* Platforms like local LGBT centers, online forums, or harm-reduction groups offer alternatives to chemsex gatherings, giving men a sense of community that doesn't revolve around substances. For those grappling with porn overuse, open dialogue with friends or a counselor—discussing how to reduce reliance on fantasy scripts—can alleviate shame and reaffirm that real-life closeness is still possible and far more rewarding in the long run.

In short, chemsex and porn may provide fleeting boosts for some gay men seeking an antidote to shame or loneliness, but their overuse can undercut the emotional richness that nurtures genuine relationships. By exploring the root causes—like internalized homophobia, body insecurities, or trauma triggers—and by seeking help where needed, men can chart a path back to deeper, more mindful intimacy. Far from moral condemnation, it's an invitation to value the quiet, sustained closeness that far outlasts the ephemeral rush of any substance or screen.

The shame spiral

When chemsex or porn consumption becomes excessive, a shame spiral often follows. A man might wake from a night of chemically charged hook-ups feeling empty, or exit a lengthy porn session hit by guilt and loneliness. This shame can dovetail with the preexisting stigma many gay men (cis or trans) endure—homophobia, transphobia, or internalized beliefs that "something is wrong" with them. According to Mustanski, Newcomb, and Garofalo (2011), unresolved shame intensifies the risk of maladaptive coping behaviors, creating a destructive loop: after feeling shame, a person might reach again for the same quick fix to numb the discomfort, and the cycle perpetuates.

Why gay men are especially impacted

Gay men in particular—many of whom grew up hiding their orientation, facing rejection from family or religious communities—may be more prone to chasing external validation. Minority stress theory (Meyer 2003) highlights how repeated discrimination fosters chronic stress and a vulnerability to negative coping strategies (see Chapter 5). If your earliest messages about desire were laced with condemnation—"It's not natural," "You're going to hell," or "Stop being so girly"—then the pull of an instant chemical or visual "escape" can feel irresistible. Chemsex can momentarily quiet that voice telling you you're unworthy; porn can provide a fantasy world where shame has no bearing. But neither fully addresses the underlying sense of invisibility or internalized homophobia.

For trans gay men, the tension can be even more pronounced. They may already battle body dysphoria or endure microaggressions in gay social circles that question their "realness" as men. Chemsex might offer a fleeting sense of confidence, enabling them to avoid deeper conversations about their bodies. Meanwhile, porn's narrow depictions of male bodies rarely match trans men's realities, risking further alienation. Studies on trans mental health (e.g., James *et al.* 2016) indicate that repeated invalidations compound stress levels, making quick-fix behaviors even more tempting as a means to sidestep emotional pain.

Disconnected encounters: eroding the capacity for true intimacy

When chemsex or porn usage dominates, the "high" or "fantasy" can overshadow gentle, mutual exploration—the kind that fosters a steady, empathic closeness. In a sex act fueled by stimulants, we might overlook a partner's subtle hints, like a nervous laugh or hesitation. We become fixated on our own amplified sensations. Similarly, in porn-driven scenarios, we might unconsciously adopt "scripts" that revolve around one-sided pleasure, ignoring spontaneous emotional signals that could lead to genuine bonding. Over time, these patterns degrade the foundation of deeper trust and hamper the ability to read a partner's emotional or physical state.

There may be relationship fallout, where partners might feel sidelined, unseen, or objectified. One might ask, "Do you want me, or do you just want that porn moment you keep chasing?" or "Is it me you want to be with, or the rush you feel on meth?" Communication breaks down when each partner remains in a separate reality—one intoxicated or fixated on a fantasy, and the other feeling neglected or confused.

Pathways to healthier connections

- *Identify emotional triggers:* Reflect on the emotional states—stress, boredom, loneliness—that precede your turn to chemsex or porn. A short log in your phone can reveal patterns, linking certain moods or conflicts to the quick fix.

- *Seek tailored support:* If chemsex is recurring, specialized resources exist, such as LGBTQ+-friendly 12-step groups or harm-reduction services that understand gay men's cultural context. The Terrence Higgins Trust (2018) also encourages safer "chillouts" or alternative social outlets less reliant on substances. For problematic porn use, consider a therapist familiar with sexual compulsions or a support group that addresses how porn might overshadow real-life intimacy.

- *Reintroduce mindful pleasure:* Gradual steps can help men reconnect with sober, present desire. Sensate-focused exercises—where you touch your partner (or yourself) gently, focusing on sensation rather than orgasm—reset the mind–body link. Over time, that rewiring can reclaim the subtle joys of real intimacy, which rely on noticing each other's cues rather than performing an idealized script. If you are single, mindful self-touch can reveal how your body responds without chemical or artificial illusions.

- *Allow for open, judgment-free conversations:* If you're partnered, addressing chemsex or heavy porn usage can be daunting. But honest discussions about how these habits affect trust, self-esteem, or physical safety can plant seeds for collaborative change. One partner might say, "I feel shut out when you watch porn for hours," or "I fear you're risking your health with these chemsex parties, and I want to help you find another release." Approaching the topic with empathy rather than condemnation fosters a supportive environment.

- *Build an alternative community:* Isolation often drives men to chemsex gatherings or to retreat into porn. Finding or creating spaces that encourage genuine conversation—be it a queer reading group, a sports league, or a Discord server that's not sexually oriented—can replace the sense of belonging once found in high-fueled or fantasy-driven escapism. Meyer's (2003) minority stress framework underscores how social networks that affirm someone's orientation or gender identity provide buffers against harmful coping methods.

Reclaiming deeper, more present intimacy

Ultimately, recognizing chemsex or porn overuse isn't a matter of moral condemnation but an invitation to value genuine closeness over fleeting highs. By acknowledging the root—maybe internalized shame, an unfulfilled desire for acceptance, or a longing for effortless self-confidence—gay men can steer away from ephemeral rushes that leave them hollow the next day. With professional help or community support, they can gradually reconnect with their authentic capacity for intimacy, finding ways to be present, collaborative, and empathic during sex rather than racing through orchestrated scripts or substance-driven illusions.

If you sense your chemsex or porn habits overshadow real-life bonds—leading to guilt, missed emotional cues, or an inability to relate authentically—consider small steps: journaling triggers, attending a single support meeting, or lowering usage for a set period to see how you feel. Over time, these adjustments pave the way for a more grounded approach to intimacy—one where empathy, tenderness, and real bodily presence displace the chaotic pursuit of chemical or digital fantasies. And in that shift, genuine sexual and emotional fulfillment may finally bloom, unmasked by ephemeral highs or harmful self-judgment.

Potential pitfalls—and how to navigate them

Having examined how chemsex and porn can erode genuine closeness if used as a stand-in for actual vulnerability, we turn now to other common pitfalls that can arise as we strive for deeper emotional and physical intimacy. Even with the best intentions, we may unwittingly sabotage closeness through unbalanced disclosures, sudden shutdowns, or neglecting key aspects of our identity (or our partner's). Recognizing these pitfalls and taking conscious steps to address them can keep our path toward meaningful connection clear, especially in a gay context that often encourages us to hide "weakness" or keep certain topics taboo.

Oversharing too soon

Why it happens

In the excitement of a budding relationship or newfound friendship, it's natural to crave immediate emotional depth. You may have felt starved for real conversation or acceptance, particularly if you're trans and found your earlier experiences invalidating. Eager for closeness, you might drop your entire life story on a new acquaintance or date, hoping they'll confirm your worth.

Consequences

Flooding someone with personal details can overwhelm them. According to communication research (Altman and Taylor 1973), relationships tend to deepen in gradual, reciprocal layers of self-disclosure—akin to peeling an onion. Jumping too many layers at once can unsettle the other person, making them pull away. You may also sense regret later, fearing you've overexposed vulnerabilities.

A healthier approach

Try a *measured disclosure strategy*. Reveal small pieces of your emotional history, then pause to see if the other person reciprocates or seems comfortable. For instance, if you mention how a family member reacted to your orientation, watch if they show empathy or curiosity. If they respond well, you can take a further step. If not, you might decide to hold back until mutual trust grows. This approach respects both your inner life and the other person's capacity to engage.

Emotional shutdown

Why it happens

For those leaning toward a dismissive-avoidant attachment style or who've been conditioned to see vulnerability as dangerous (common among gay men who faced ridicule for being "too emotional"), shutting down feels protective. When a partner or friend shows strong feelings—crying about stress, revealing a deep fear—you might interpret it as an invasion of your autonomy.

Consequences

Withdrawal can undercut intimacy, leaving the other person feeling invalidated or alone. In longitudinal studies on adult attachment (Simpson and Rholes 2017), repeated emotional stonewalling consistently predicts dissatisfaction. Over time, the shutdown partner builds resentment or thinks you don't care, driving a wedge between you.

A healthier approach

Instead of fleeing, *name your discomfort*: "I'm feeling uneasy hearing so much emotion, but I want to stay present if I can."

If it's too overwhelming, suggest a short break—like a 5-minute pause to gather your thoughts—then return to the conversation. This compromise prevents you from vanishing and signals willingness to support the other person, even if it's challenging.

Failing to address dysphoria or gender identity

Why it happens

In relationships where one partner is trans, or you're the trans individual, both sides may hesitate to discuss transition details, pronouns, or bodily changes—worried about saying "the wrong thing." Alternatively, the cis partner may overfixate, turning the trans partner into a curiosity. Both extremes—complete avoidance or invasive hyper-focus—undermine trust and closeness.

Consequences

Ignoring dysphoria means the trans partner's core experiences remain invisible, fostering resentment or shame. Overfixating can feel like objectification. For example, if you're always checking your partner's scars or focusing conversation on "how your transition is going," you risk overshadowing the person's broader emotional life.

A healthier approach

Balanced communication is key. If you're cis and want to understand your trans partner's reality, ask gentle, respectful questions, but also take initiative to learn from resources (e.g., books, online articles). If you're trans, clarify boundaries: "I'm okay discussing my chest scars, but let's not make it the centerpiece of every conversation." This fosters an environment where your trans identity is acknowledged without being the sole focus, letting you grow intimacy in all other facets too.

Expecting intimacy to cure trauma

Why it happens

We often romanticize closeness as a balm for all psychological wounds—assuming that if we just find "the right partner" or get emotional enough, our deeper traumas will vanish. For gay men who've endured harsh condemnation, this longing for a healing relationship is understandable. But it can place an unrealistic burden on intimacy to fix everything.

Consequences

Intimacy can certainly be therapeutic, but if we rely on a partner or friend to resolve entrenched trauma, we risk disappointment and may strain the relationship. Clinical psychology research (Cloitre *et al.* 2019) emphasizes that while supportive connections aid recovery, severe traumas (such as repeated bullying or homophobic abuse) often require specialized interventions—like trauma-focused therapy.

A healthier approach

View closeness as *complementary* to professional help, not a substitute. If you sense your trauma responses are overwhelming—for instance, panic attacks or flashbacks—seek a therapist trained in LGBTQ+ trauma. Let your partner or friend be an ally, not your only lifeline. This balanced approach means you enjoy the emotional benefits of intimacy while addressing the deeper causes of your distress in a structured, safe environment.

Overlooking relationship structures (monogamy vs. open/poly)

Why it happens

Gay communities sometimes normalize open or polyamorous relationships, while others hold monogamy as nonnegotiable. If you and your partner never openly discuss your preferences—one craving monogamy to feel secure, the other craving openness for sexual variety—tension simmers beneath the surface.

Consequences

Unspoken misalignment can corrode closeness through guilt, resentment, or fear of losing the relationship. If you lie or hide interactions outside the relationship, a sense of betrayal may erupt later. Conversely, if one partner feels coerced into an open setup, emotional safety diminishes.

A healthier approach

Transparent discussion about relationship formats fosters clarity. Maybe you set boundaries like "We only play together," or "We can see others, but we always tell each other first." This dialogue can also be a time to disclose vulnerabilities—like, "I'm worried I'm not enough for you" or "I fear being suffocated by monogamy." Even if irreconcilable differences emerge, handling them openly is more respectful than letting resentment fester in silence.

Having explored these pitfalls—from oversharing to ignoring major identity aspects—the next logical step is to consider how *emotional and physical intimacy* can be consciously woven together. Rather than letting these pitfalls derail closeness, we can proactively structure our approach to intimacy with thoughtful pacing, clear communication, and a willingness to embrace awkward moments as part of the journey.

Bridging emotional and physical intimacy

Moving from potential pitfalls into *positive, proactive strategies,* we now examine how to align emotional openness with physical closeness, ensuring neither is neglected. For gay men, especially those who carry body insecurities or complex identities, bridging the emotional and the sexual demands intentional effort—balancing caution with curiosity, speed with sincerity.

Gradual pacing for comfort

Why emotional safety first?

Many men dive into sexual territory swiftly, sometimes mistaking intense physical chemistry for deeper intimacy. While a quick fling can be enjoyable, if you seek a more soul-nourishing bond, building emotional safety ahead of or alongside sexual exploration can enhance trust. Relationship research (Reis and Shaver 1988; Reis, Clark, and Holmes 2004) shows that couples who disclose feelings progressively often report higher satisfaction.

Practical steps

Share reflections on your day—joys, stresses, fleeting anxieties—before attempting complex sexual acts. Over time, these daily glimpses form an emotional bedrock. When you do transition to more intimate physical activities, there's already a sense of mutual understanding. If you are single, practicing open sharing with friends fosters the habit of vulnerability, so you're not caught off-guard when a new partner emerges.

Verbalizing emotions before touch

Why clear communication matters

If you hope to try a new position or show a part of your body you've been self-conscious about—scars, a disability, or the results of gender-affirming surgery—openly stating your curiosity or anxiety can lighten the tension for both you and your partner.

Practical steps

"I'm intrigued by using a harness, but I'm nervous because I've never done it" or "I had top surgery; I want you to see my chest, but I also feel apprehensive." This direct approach transforms potential awkwardness into collaborative care. If you're single, mentally rehearsing how you'd voice these concerns prepares you for a real conversation down the line, enabling calmness instead of panic.

Embracing awkwardness

Why perfectionism undermines closeness

Gay men often absorb messages that sex should look and feel "flawless," possibly influenced by curated porn or peers who boast about seamless encounters. Yet real intimacy overflows with small "mistakes:" a squeak, a miscommunication, a foot cramp mid-position change.

Practical tip

Laugh it off—"That definitely wasn't in the script!"—and proceed. This acceptance fosters a playful energy that can deepen the bond. Laughter dispels shame, reminding you both that you're not performing a show; you're engaged in a mutual experience. Over time, these comedic slipups can become tender, lighthearted moments you both remember—small threads of shared history that soften future vulnerabilities.

With these bridging strategies—emotional safety, direct communication, and relaxed acceptance of imperfection—we set the stage for a deeper, more fulfilling closeness. Now let's illustrate how these principles come to life by visiting Tomas and Adam, weaving both emotional and physical intimacy with mindful awareness.

INTEGRATING CLOSENESS

Tomas (mid-thirties, trans gay man) moved to a more accepting city hoping to leave behind old prejudices. Adam (late twenties, cis gay man) was raised in a progressive household but wrestles with ingrained insecurities about "acting masculine enough." Tomas and Adam have dated for about a month.

The emotional step

Over dinner, Adam suggests, "Tell me something real about your day—like, genuinely real." Tomas exhales, then confides that his coworker made a microaggressive remark, implying that "being trans and gay is asking for double trouble." Adam quietly reaches for Tomas's hand, replying, "I'm so sorry that happened. That must have hurt. Tell me more if you want." Tomas feels a sense of relief—someone acknowledging his intersectional identity without minimization. This exchange fosters emotional trust, reinforcing a sense that it's safe to reveal more.

Transition to physical closeness

Later that evening, they lounge on Adam's sofa. Adam begins to stroke Tomas's hair, but senses a fleeting stiffness. Tomas halts him with a small gesture, eyes brimming with uncertainty. "I'm still self-conscious about my chest scars," he admits. "Sometimes I'm afraid they'll scare you off." Adam responds softly, "Thank you for sharing that. How would you feel about dimming the lights, or leaving your shirt on until you're comfortable?" A wave of relief washes through Tomas. Instead of pushing or trivializing, Adam meets him with patience and empathy. In that moment, the emotional closeness they nurtured over dinner flows seamlessly into physical intimacy—a gentle synergy of trust, honesty, and mutual respect.

Outcome

In that single evening, they practice every bridging skill mentioned: gradually unveiling deeper feelings, naming emotions before physical exploration, and embracing potential awkwardness about scars or bodily changes. The result is a more integrated closeness—less a performance, more a conversation. They realize that these small steps can multiply over time, forging a bond that acknowledges who Tomas is, scars and all, and who Adam is, insecurities included.

Drawing it all together

Trust as the soil, intimacy as the seed

As Chapter 5 detailed, *trust* is the fertile bed from which deeper connections can grow. Now, we've seen how *intimacy*—both emotional and physical—can root itself in that soil, blossoming into a bond that merges honesty, empathy, and shared vulnerability. An anxious heart might find steady acceptance, an avoidant mind might learn to stay present, and a trans man wary of scars might discover that they can be gently embraced rather than hidden away.

Evolving patterns over time

No single technique or conversation cements intimacy permanently. It's an ongoing cycle: each time you name a fear, invite your partner's perspective, or explore new bodily sensations with mindful checks, you deepen closeness. Over repeated experiences, patterns shift. A once-avoidant person becomes more open to requests for emotional support, an anxious partner learns to breathe through the moment instead of demanding constant reassurance, and a trans man uncertain about his chest or genital configuration finds confidence in a partner's consistent warmth. Like forest growth, these changes accumulate slowly but meaningfully.

Pitfalls, progress, and playfulness

Triggers and doubts can still materialize when we least expect them, reminding us of old traumas or fresh insecurities. By naming them—"That touched on an old wound"—we reclaim control. This process helps us see ourselves not as burdened by our orientation or identity, but as *dynamic individuals* forging resilient connections. Meanwhile, sprinkling in moments of *genuine playfulness*—laughing at a silly mishap in bed or telling a partner, "You look hilariously adorable right now"—helps keep the emotional climate buoyant.

MAPPING YOUR INTIMACY FOREST

To internalize these concepts, consider a creative activity that externalizes your emotional experiences.

Draw your forest path

On a blank page, sketch a meandering trail that symbolizes your journey toward deeper intimacy. Label the "clearings" where you feel safe (e.g., "Laughing with best friends," "Feeling confident post-workout," "Sharing a worry with a partner"). Also mark the "shadows" (e.g., "Fear of not being masculine enough," "Dysphoria around chest or scars," "Worry about HIV status").

Identify allies and tools

Around the path, add simple icons or notes representing your resources: a "cabin" labeled "Therapy," a bright sun labeled "Supportive mentor," a well labeled "Self-compassion." This highlights that you aren't navigating the forest alone; you have guides, be they professionals, friends, or personal practices.

Pick a shadow to address

In a journal, select one area of the trail that feels daunting—maybe body shame, an old heartbreak, or a conflict about relationship structure. Write about how you could move closer to it safely, perhaps by confiding in a therapist, friend, or potential partner. If you are single, consider how you might approach future relationships with mindful vulnerability.

Why it works: Seeing your emotional topography in a tangible form helps you recognize that the forest isn't uniformly dark. Clearings of confidence exist, as do supportive resources. Acknowledging these can reduce the sense of being lost or helpless, spurring actionable steps that gradually reduce your fear and expand your capacity for closeness.

Small, honest moments as the seeds of true closeness: the ongoing path

Whether you're single, partnered, cis, or trans, each of us harbors a natural longing to be seen and cherished in our true form. Yet many of us, bearing the scars of harsh judgments or abandonment, reflexively recoil at the idea of letting down our guard. This chapter shows that *intimacy*—the blending of emotional openness and physical responsiveness—does indeed ask us to tread into vulnerable territory. Still, it also offers the richest experiences of communion, comfort, and mutual growth.

Perhaps you'll begin by voicing a small anxiety to a friend or new date, or by unveiling a piece of your physical self you've long hidden. If you're in a relationship, you might schedule a weekly "intimacy hour," exploring tender topics or playful new physical gestures. If you're a trans gay man, clarifying which aspects of your transition you're ready to share can reshape your partner's approach, ensuring you remain in control of your narrative. If you've leaned on chemsex or porn as a crutch, you might revisit the habits, noticing whether they hamper the emotional presence you crave, and consider small, supportive shifts or professional assistance.

Recall that no great intimacy occurs in a single leap; it's a mosaic composed of *small, honest moments*. Each tender admission—"I'm scared," "I'm curious," "I have these scars"—and each empathetic response—"I hear you," "I'm here"—threads another stitch in the tapestry of genuine closeness. Awkward misfires, comedic slipups, or uncomfortable truths become less threatening when approached with acceptance. Over time, you may find your orientation, your trans identity, your unique body, and your entire personal backstory not as burdens to be concealed, but as integral parts of who you are—capable of offering and receiving profound warmth.

And if triggers or old insecurities flare up, remember the *self-compassion* and *trust-building strategies* from earlier chapters: breathe, name the feeling, assure yourself that you're allowed this process. By refusing to let shame or fear dictate the story, you grant intimacy the space to blossom in the present. May each small opening—every admission of a hidden fear, every gentle affirmation from a partner—draw you farther along the path toward the robust, affirming closeness you wholeheartedly deserve.

CHAPTER 7

Turning Toward Each Other and Communicating with Care

I used to believe that *grand gestures*—like writing a heartfelt love letter or planning an extravagant getaway—held the real power to keep relationships afloat. Certainly, these moments can be profoundly meaningful. Yet, in my late twenties, I started noticing that many of my gay friends, clients, and even myself were falling into a specific trap: we'd expend a massive effort on these occasional big expressions of love or attention, but *neglect the tiny, everyday points of contact* that truly underlie closeness. Over time, I realized that a single shining weekend trip to the coast meant far less if the day-to-day, minute-to-minute communication was riddled with sarcasm, dismissiveness, or half-listening.

As Dr. John Gottman's research famously shows (Gottman and Silver 1999), *little daily interactions*—the way we respond to a sigh, the tone we use when our partner is stressed—actually form the "heartbeat" of the relationship. In my own life, I've seen how a seemingly trivial comment ("You're always so dramatic") can cut deeper for gay men, especially those of us who grew up hearing we weren't "masculine enough" or were "too sensitive." For trans gay men, subtle remarks about body or identity can similarly land with amplified force, serving as a painful echo of earlier invalidations from friends, family, or entire communities.

This chapter assembles everything we've learned about trauma, self-compassion, trust, and intimacy into tangible communication practices. We'll dig into how to notice and respond to emotional bids, explore Dr. Gottman's "four horsemen," apply direct exercises to break negative loops, and see how to foster emotional safety in our daily lives. These tools aren't for "instant fixes" but for incremental growth. Feel free to pause reading when you feel overwhelmed, let insights settle, and then return to apply them bit by bit. Over time, these skills can reshape how you show up in relationships—whether with a longtime partner, a new romantic interest, or even a trusted friend or mentor.

A deeper journey into the forest of dialogue

Where we've been so far

This book has walked you through multiple layers of personal and relational healing:

- Chapters 1 and 2 addressed how trauma shapes our emotional reflexes and how minority stress or family rejection add extra layers of vulnerability.
- Chapter 3 introduced attachment styles—secure, anxious-preoccupied, dismissive-avoidant, and fearful-avoidant (disorganized)—revealing how formative experiences shape adult relationships.

- Chapter 4 covered self-compassion, a crucial tool for gay men who often internalize shame or microaggressions.
- Chapter 5 focused on trust: how it forms, how it's eroded, and why consistent empathy matters so deeply for those who have endured homophobia, transphobia, or half-hearted family acceptance.
- Chapter 6 delved into emotional and sexual intimacy, illustrating how vulnerability deepens connection and can help us unlearn shame.

Now, in Chapter 7, we integrate these insights into *daily communication*—the actual process of speaking, listening, and responding that either cements trust or gradually dismantles it. You might imagine we've ventured into an older, denser part of the forest: the vines (old hurts, cultural pressures) can snag us, yet the soil here is rich and brimming with potential, if we tread attentively.

This chapter is lengthy because communication is multifaceted. We'll examine spotting emotional bids, turning toward versus turning away, fostering emotional safety, Dr. John Gottman's "four horsemen," and some common pitfalls with their solutions. Consider reading one or two sections at a time, reflecting on how they apply to your situation, and then returning for more. The goal isn't perfection but gradual internalization of these patterns.

Why communication matters even more for gay men

Societal scrutiny and conditional acceptance

Many gay men have grown up under a magnifying glass, constantly aware that family or society might disapprove of how we speak, dress, or express emotion. This scrutiny can manifest in subtle forms—like a coworker's "You seem different"—to overt hostility in deeply conservative regions or religious communities. Well-intentioned family might say, "We accept you, but please don't bring your partner to the reunion," a conditional acceptance that fosters anxiety about truly being ourselves.

Such experiences prime us to scan every conversation for the risk of criticism or rejection. We wonder, *Will I be too flamboyant if I laugh out loud? Too needy if I admit anxiety?* Over time, these self-monitoring behaviors can warp how we communicate in close relationships. We might:

- Stay silent when upset, fearing a negative reaction
- Overcompensate with humor or sarcasm rather than genuine vulnerability
- Dismiss emotional signals from others because it's safer than engaging.

Communication as the daily heartbeat

In the grand scheme of building or maintaining a relationship—be it a casual dating scenario, a deep friendship, or a long-term partnership—*communication* is the minute-to-minute practice that underlies trust, intimacy, and conflict resolution. Even if you're not romantically involved, these skills shape how you relate to your chosen family, best friends, or even potential mentors. As homophobia or transphobia can erode our baseline sense of safety, the ability to communicate with consistent warmth and presence becomes a powerful healing force.

Spotting emotional bids: the small invitations that guide connection

What are emotional bids?

Dr. John Gottman, famous for his "Love Lab" research,[1] observed that couples who flourish regularly engage in "bids for connection." An emotional bid can be as modest as a quick question—"How was your day?"—or as overt as "I feel sad right now; can we talk?" The essence is a *desire for attention or empathy*. A typical day is filled with potential emotional bids: a friend sighs, "Work was rough," a partner says, "Look at this hilarious meme," or a roommate casually remarks, "I'm feeling kind of lonely tonight." Each instance is a small nudge seeking your engagement.

For gay men who faced ridicule or were told "Men shouldn't be emotional," these bids can be tricky to spot or respond to. You might have learned from your teenage years that expressing emotional needs is "feminine," "weak," or "too dramatic," leading you to either *hide* your own bids or *ignore* others'. Relearning to notice them—and respond warmly to them—becomes key to forging deeper bonds.

Why emotional bids are often overlooked or misread

There are plenty of reasons why emotional bids slip by unseen:

- *Distraction:* In a world of phone pings, streaming services, and busy careers, we're often mentally elsewhere.
- *Personal insecurities:* If we worry about being "too needy,"

1 www.gottman.com/love-lab

we may not voice an emotional bid in the first place, or we interpret someone else's as burdensome.

- *Cultural norms:* Families or communities that discourage emotional talk can produce adults who rarely label their feelings.
- *Intersectional pressures:* If you're a Deaf gay man and others fail to use sign language, or if you're a gay man of color suspecting that others don't see your experiences of racism as valid, you may stop making emotional bids altogether, feeling invisible.

Turning toward vs. turning away: choices that accumulate

When someone shares a concern—or even a lighthearted remark—the listener tends to respond in one of three ways:

- *Turning toward:* Engaging, "Let's talk about that. I want to understand."
- *Turning away:* Ignoring or half-responding, "Uh-huh, yeah," while scrolling on their phone.
- *Turning against:* Offering a mocking or hostile reply, "You're so sensitive."

The dynamic drastically changes depending on which route you choose. For example, if a date quietly says, "I'm anxious about meeting your friends," turning away or against may confirm their fear that their feelings aren't taken seriously. On the other hand, turning toward fosters closeness. One moment might seem tiny, but repeated day after day, these responses define the bond's emotional climate.

The emotional bank account

Gottman uses the *emotional bank account* metaphor[2] to illustrate how each positive, empathetic response is a deposit, and each dismissive or negative reaction is a withdrawal. Over time, consistent deposits lead to a healthy surplus, meaning that when stress or a conflict arises, you have enough goodwill to handle it without catastrophic breakdown.

For single gay men, this practice starts long before a committed relationship. It can mean noticing and engaging with friends' bids, choosing to say, "Tell me more about that stressful meeting," instead of brushing them off with "I'm busy, sorry." It can also apply in dating: replying warmly to a playful text, showing genuine interest when someone shares a story, or following up on something they mentioned last time you spoke. These small acts of turning toward build the reflexes that will help sustain a future partnership.

For couples, the same principle applies in the rhythms of daily life. A "How did you sleep?" in the morning, a genuine greeting when you return home, or an offer to help with dinner are all deposits that strengthen the emotional core. When bigger challenges, like disagreements about money, sex, or family, arise, the positive balance you've built makes it far more likely you'll approach them with cooperation instead of defensiveness.

Everyday contexts where emotional bids appear

We might not notice how often emotional bids surface in daily life. With roommates or chosen family, a comment like "The neighbor's dog barked all night" can be met with validation, "That's tough, are you feeling exhausted?", or with a shrug

2 www.gottman.com/blog/invest-relationship-emotional-bank-account?

and "Oh well," which inadvertently turns away. On dating apps, a new match might say, "I just moved here, feel clueless." Turning toward could sound like, "I'd be happy to share some tips about the local gay scene," transforming a casual opener into a personal connection. Even within family relationships, the same principle applies. If an aunt calls with a gentle, "Are you okay? You sound down," you could respond with openness, "I've been stressed, but let's talk", or shut the door with a brisk "I'm fine, no big deal." In each case, the choice to turn toward or away can subtly shift the tone and trajectory of the relationship.

Repair attempts for missed emotional bids

Even if you initially turn away—distracted by your phone or your own thoughts—an immediate or near-immediate *repair attempt* can restore connection. For instance, "Sorry, I was zoned out. You said you had a rough day—tell me more?" That small apology plus renewed attention reopens a door that was about to close. If you realize hours later you brushed someone off, you might text or call them back, acknowledging your slip.

Emotional safety: the essential canopy over communication

Emotional safety—the sense that you can disclose thoughts and feelings without being ridiculed, shamed, or punished—forms the protective canopy under which honest communication flourishes. For many gay men, emotional safety was shaky at best if they had to conceal orientation from relatives or endure school bullying. This leaves a legacy of vigilance: *Will I be mocked if I share my real opinion? Will someone walk away if I reveal my vulnerabilities?*

A 2021 survey by the Trevor Project found that a high percentage of LGBTQ+ youth who lacked supportive familial environments displayed heightened anxiety about open communication. While youth data may not directly map onto adult gay men, the pattern underscores how deeply embedded these fears can be. If you spent adolescence anxiously minding every word at the dinner table, you might carry that into adulthood, reluctant to speak up or name your emotional needs.

Here are some common barriers to emotional safety for gay men:

- *Past bullying:* Hearing "Faggot!" or other slurs in school hallways can create a reflex where any harsh tone triggers a surge of fear or anger.
- *Family non-acceptance:* A father who insisted, "We don't talk about your lifestyle here," fosters the belief that your emotional truth is unwelcome.
- *Religious or cultural pressures:* In some faith communities, being openly gay (or trans) is seen as sinful or deviant, intensifying the fear of condemnation.

Here are some practices that foster safety:

- *Gentle honesty:* Instead of snapping "You're an idiot!" when you are feeling stressed, you might say, "I'm feeling overwhelmed and it's making me irritable. Let's slow down."
- *Validating phrases:* "I see where you're coming from," or "It makes sense you'd feel hurt by that." These small validations let a partner know they're heard.
- *Consistent respect:* Refrain from eye-rolls, sarcasm, or belittling

language. Over time, such respect reassures that you won't shame them for being human.

Consider this example. Chris (thirties, gay cis man living with HIV) contemplates telling a new friend about his status. If the friend calmly says, "Thank you for sharing. I value your honesty, and I know about U=U," Chris instantly feels safer—fear recedes because he's met with acceptance, not scorn. That moment sets a precedent for future open exchanges.

Dr. John Gottman's "four horsemen:" origins, research, and why they matter

An overview of Dr. Gottman's "Love Lab" overview

Dr. John Gottman devoted decades at the University of Washington to studying couples in a specialized environment: the so-called "Love Lab," an apartment-like setup rigged with cameras and sensors to observe interactions in real time (Gottman and Silver 2015). Researchers observed thousands of couples—eventually including same-sex partnerships—discuss everyday issues. They recorded physiologic changes (heart rate, perspiration) and microscopic facial expressions (eye-rolls, tight lips) that hint at deeper emotional states.

Over time, Dr. Gottman and his colleagues identified a set of negative interaction patterns—the "four horsemen"—that reliably predicted which couples would thrive or falter (Gottman and Silver 2015). While some might worry that this research, initially based on heterosexual couples, might not apply to gay men, subsequent expansions of the dataset and separate studies confirm that *critique*, *contempt*, *defensiveness*, and *stonewalling* cut across all orientations. The emotional dynamics—empathy, warmth, negative escalation—are profoundly similar in shaping relationship satisfaction.

Harsh critique vs. constructive complaint

Harsh critique directly assaults character, framing a person as flawed: "You're so selfish!" or "You're always lazy." By targeting who they are rather than addressing what they did, this provokes shame or anger. Dr. Gottman's footage often shows a quick escalation after harsh critique—heart rates spike, voices rise, and problem-solving becomes minimal (Gottman 2023).

For gay men, critique can easily echo old anxieties about being "not man enough" or "too flamboyant." A partner snapping, "Why do you always act so dramatic?" might reopen teenage wounds. The constructive alternative is a focused complaint: naming the behavior, not the person. Instead of "You're lazy," one partner says, "I feel frustrated that the dishes are piling up—can we handle them tonight?"

Contempt: the single strongest predictor of relationship failure

Contempt stands out as the deadliest horseman, according to Dr. Gottman's longitudinal research (Gottman and Silver 1999). Eye-rolling, sneers, or belittling remarks like "You're pathetic" or "You disgust me" convey moral or intellectual superiority. Among gay men who endured systematic invalidation, a contemptuous comment can reawaken the feeling of *I'm worthless in this person's eyes*. Repeated contempt fosters deep resentment, corroding any sense of emotional safety.

The antidote is direct respect: even in anger, articulate the frustration without belittling your partner's worth. For example, "I'm upset about how we're handling money, but I know you're trying. Let's figure out a strategy."

Defensiveness: blocking connection

Defensiveness arises when we feel accused. We might retort, "Don't blame me; you're the one who's wrong!" or shift blame entirely, "Well, you do that too!" Dr. Gottman discovered that such knee-jerk self-protection halts real resolution, turning each disagreement into a blame game (Gottman and Silver 1999).

For gay men, if the world has often told you "You're at fault for being gay," you might be hyper-alert to criticism, interpreting any small complaint as another condemnation. The solution is empathetic ownership: "I see I contributed to this confusion. Let's fix it." That stance frees both parties to address the issue cooperatively.

Stonewalling: the silent treatment that undercuts security

Stonewalling is shutting down entirely—heart pounding, mind racing, but outwardly silent or aloof. The other person feels abandoned, potentially panics, and pursues more. This chase-and-flee cycle can intensify quickly. Stonewalling is especially common among those who feel overwhelmed by conflict, who see no safe path except to disengage.

A 20-minute break or "I need a moment to calm down" is vital for recentering. The key difference: you promise to come back and actually do so, ensuring your partner or friend knows the conversation isn't permanently closed.

Common pitfalls and solutions for day-to-day challenges

Dr. Gottman's "four horsemen" (Gottman and Silver 1999) describe four destructive communication patterns—criticism, contempt, defensiveness, and stonewalling—that predict relationship breakdown. Now let's address typical daily hurdles that can sabotage effective communication, especially for gay men.

External stress seeping in

You might work in a mostly straight environment, hearing microaggressions—like "Oh, my gay best friend is so funny"—implying you should be comedic relief. Or your boss cracks a "lighthearted" homophobic joke. Arriving home, you're tense, snapping at your partner or roommate over minor matters (like a misplaced remote). This is "kick the dog syndrome." Name the real stress: "I'm irritable because a coworker made a snide remark about gay men today." That direct statement turns potential conflict into shared empathy, allowing the other person to support you instead of feeling attacked.

Additional minority stressors

Communication breakdown can occur when intersectional identities aren't acknowledged. A Deaf gay man might find that his hearing partner rarely makes an effort to sign or slow down speech, leaving him feeling turned away from daily conversations. A gay man of color living with a white partner might repeatedly sense his partner diminishing concerns about microaggressions or racism, leading to frustration.

When Cyrus's coworkers refer to "urban flamboyant styles," they use coded language that merges racial and homophobic stereotypes. "Urban" often implies "Black, Latino, or otherwise non-white," while "flamboyant" suggests "excessively gay or effeminate." The subtext? "Your manner of expression isn't welcome in a professional environment." For Cyrus (thirties, Black cis gay man), that remark is more than mild annoyance: it echoes centuries of stereotypes policing how Black men "ought" to behave (stoic, masculine, subdued). Returning home to Jude (late twenties, Cyrus's roommate), Cyrus is seething, but Jude initially wonders if Cyrus is just "in a mood." Once they name the deeper intersectional wound—"They basically said I'm 'too Black, too gay' to fit in"—the conversation can shift from friction about chores to mutual support.

Avoiding big topics to "keep the peace"

Major relationship questions—like whether to have children, to have an open relationship, or relocate—can loom unspoken if you fear stirring conflict. But burying these differences rarely works; tensions eventually erupt. Engaging them with gentle startups—for example, "I value us. Can we calmly talk about our parenting views?"—fosters clarity. If stress spikes, take breaks but continue until you reach a workable resolution or at least an understanding. Some couples may decide they're incompatible, which, while painful, is more respectful than living in silent tension.

Sexual communication breakdowns

Sex can become an emotional minefield if expectations diverge or if personal insecurities stay hidden:

- Performance anxiety: "Am I lasting long enough?"
- Mismatched libido: "You want it daily, I'm fine with weekly."
- Body insecurities: "I feel I'm not masculine enough" or "My scars bother me."

In gay men's spaces, including trans men, these concerns can intensify if we feel pressured by porn-inspired ideals, toxic masculinity, or a desire to prove our sexual prowess. A mindful approach, like "Let's spend 20 minutes on non-goal-oriented touching, then share any feelings that arise," can melt shame or fear. For single men, discussing these topics with a trusted friend or therapist can build ease for future intimate scenarios.

Digital overreliance: screens in bed

Ever tried talking to a partner who's glued to their phone? You might sense your words bouncing off a wall. In an era of countless digital distractions, missed bids abound. A friend sighs, "I had the worst day," but we're too absorbed in group chats to notice. Reinstating device-free zones—like the hour before sleep or during dinner—lets you observe each other's subtle emotional cues, bridging closeness that might otherwise slip away.

Exercises and rituals for lasting change

Knowing what fosters or derails effective communication is one thing; doing it consistently requires practice. Here are some structured methods to develop communication habits—adaptable for single men, those in relationships, or those living in a chosen family setup.

EMOTIONAL BIDS JOURNAL

Purpose: Train yourself to notice and respond to emotional bids.

Duration: Choose a period of 1–2 weeks.

Logging: Keep a small notebook or phone note. When you spot a potential emotional bid (someone sighing, a casual remark, a direct question), write it down.

Your response: Mark if you turned toward ("Tell me more"), away ("Oh, that's nice"), or against ("You're overreacting").

Nightly reflection: Check your list. Identify moments you handled well and those that could've gone better.

Optional share: If you trust the person, reveal your findings: "I realized when you brought up feeling lonely, I was too distracted. Sorry. Let's chat if you still feel that way."

Over time, you'll see patterns—maybe you ignore emotional bids when you're tired or stressed. Once aware, you can consciously shift toward engagement.

THE "FOUR HORSEMEN" SELF-AUDIT

Purpose: Spot when critique, contempt, defensiveness, or stonewalling sneak into your daily interactions.

Duration: Identify a period, a week or two, where you track conflicts or tense moments.

Trigger and pattern: Jot down what sparked the conflict and which horseman you used, for example, "We argued about dishes; I used *contempt* by rolling my eyes."

Antidote: Replace the negative reaction with the recommended approach (constructive complaint, respect, ownership, self-soothing).

Week's end review: See if certain times, contexts, or triggers cause consistent negative habits. Plan a better approach—like scheduling hard talks on a relaxed weekend morning rather than late at night.

This structured awareness can be eye-opening, revealing how small patterns accumulate.

EMOTIONAL SAFETY "HOME BASE" RITUAL

Purpose: Maintain a consistent sense of security in close relationships.

Duration: Set a regular time, weekly or bi-weekly, and dedicate 20–30 minutes to check emotional "vitals."

Gentle opener: "How are we doing? Are there any worries we've brushed aside?"

Use nonblaming language: Instead of "You never listen," say "I'm concerned we might be missing each other's deeper feelings."

Close positively: "I care about how you feel. Let's keep this space safe for honesty."

If you are single, adapt this for personal check-ins with a close friend or sibling, ensuring both sides feel heard.

CONFLICT DEBRIEF

Purpose: Analyze a recent argument to improve future communication, picking a manageable disagreement—not your biggest meltdown, but one that stung.

Recount: Each participant explains their perspective, including physical sensations (tense shoulders, racing heart) and emotional states (fear, anger).

Spot the "four horsemen": Did critique, contempt, defensiveness, or stonewalling appear? Acknowledge it.

Rewind and replay: Consider alternative responses—like pausing earlier or using empathic phrases.

Positive closure: Thank each other for willingness to reflect, reinforcing an atmosphere of mutual care.

SINGLE MEN'S ADAPTATION: THE "DATING DEBRIEF"

Purpose: Enhance self-awareness and skillful communication in the dating realm.

Post-date reflection: After a casual meetup, quickly note if you or the other person made emotional bids, and how each responded.

Identify patterns: Are you too quick to open up? Is the other person ignoring your attempts to connect? Do sarcasm or shallow banter predominate?

Adjust and self-compassion: If you spot repeated negativity, decide if you need better boundaries or a more discerning selection of dates. Offer yourself understanding: *Their dismissal doesn't define my worth.*

This fosters a more mindful approach to new connections, preventing repeated pitfalls.

TWO-WEEK COMMUNICATION JOURNEY

To see these practices in action, let's follow a short chronological narrative with multiple gay men, each dealing with distinct communication challenges. Over 14 days, watch how small daily decisions—turning toward or away, using the "four horsemen" or not—shape the trajectory of each situation.

Characters and context

Jude (late twenties, cis gay man, single): Recently moved to a big city post-breakup. Lives with Cyrus (forty-five, divorced), an older gay roommate, who ended a fifteen-year relationship painfully. Their dynamic is friendly yet sometimes tense.

Elias (mid-thirties, cis gay man) and Gabe (thirties, cis gay man, dating): Grappling with boundaries around Gabe's HIV-positive status and public activism.

Miguel (fifties, cis gay man): Jude's uncle, estranged from certain relatives who never embraced his orientation. Considers reconnecting with Jude's father.

Days 1–2: Setting the stage

Jude and Cyrus's missed emotional bids

Day 1, morning: Jude sighs over breakfast, "I still haven't met decent guys here. Feels hopeless." Cyrus, reading something on his phone, only half glances up. "You'll figure it out," he mumbles. Jude feels deflated. The missed emotional bid sets a tone of mild distance.

Elias and Gabe's mild stonewalling

Day 1, lunch: Gabe invites Elias to a forthcoming HIV-awareness event. Elias, anxious about possible acquaintances seeing him there, responds with mild stonewalling: "We'll see," then changes the subject. Gabe senses he's being brushed off but holds back from pushing.

Miguel, left hanging

Day 2: Miguel sends Jude a text: "Any update on your dad's birthday? Should I try contacting him?" Jude, buried in errands, ignores it until bedtime. Turning away leaves Miguel hanging, anxious about bridging the family gap alone.

Day 3: Realizing missed emotional bids

Jude and Cyrus depositing positivity

That evening, Jude tries again: "I've been feeling really stuck. Can we talk?" Cyrus, noticing his earlier brush-off, sets the phone aside: "Sure. I'm listening." Jude opens up about heartbreak from his last relationship, how the city feels overwhelming. Cyrus empathizes, turning toward him this time, depositing a bit of positivity into the emotional bank.

Elias and Gabe's mild hesitation

At dinner, Gabe repeats: "The HIV event is in two weeks; I'd love for us to go together." Elias, not fully stonewalling now, expresses mild hesitation: "I'm worried who might see me. Let's talk about it later." They leave it unresolved, but at least Gabe doesn't feel outright dismissed.

Miguel taking action

Miguel calls Jude about the ignored text. Jude apologizes, admitting he was swamped and didn't realize how worried Miguel might be. They schedule a call for the weekend to discuss father-related tensions more thoroughly.

Days 4–5: Conflict patterns and the "four horsemen" appear

Jude and Cyrus recalling Dr. Gottman's "four horsemen"

Day 4: Jude forgets to tidy the kitchen after cooking. Cyrus returns from a difficult day at work, sees the mess, and snaps: "Why are you so lazy?" This is *harsh critique*, labeling Jude's character instead of addressing the immediate behavior. Jude fires back defensively: "That's not fair—I planned to clean soon!" Right there, critique and defensiveness clash. Mid-argument, Cyrus recalls Dr. Gottman's distinction between "You never do chores!" and "I'm upset because I came home to a messy kitchen." He tries to pivot: "Okay, sorry I called you lazy. I'm just stressed. Can we set a schedule so I'm not worrying daily?" Tension eases; they salvage the moment by adopting a more constructive tone.

Elias and Gabe, naming negative patterns

Day 5: Gabe again nudges Elias about the HIV event. Elias feels cornered, blurting: "Why do you always push me into these things?" edging toward contempt or critique. Gabe, hurt, calls it out: "That feels like you're belittling me for caring. Can we slow down?" They both step back before it escalates. Although unresolved, naming the negative pattern spares them from deeper harm.

Miguel's mild stonewalling

Mulling over Jude's father's birthday is nerve-wracking. Miguel calls Jude, but mid-conversation, he veers off to a trivial topic, practicing a mild form of *stonewalling*. The fear of rejection is so intense he can't talk about it. Jude senses the abrupt shift, feeling confused. They realize ignoring it won't help, so they vow to keep addressing it in small increments.

Days 6–7: Repair attempts and emotional safety gains

Jude and Cyrus's conflict debrief

Day 6: Jude and Cyrus hold a brief "conflict debrief" about the kitchen flare-up. Cyrus acknowledges his harsh day at work spiked his irritability. Jude notes he still feels raw from the breakup. They agree to state external stress whenever they feel edgy: "Work was brutal today" or "I'm feeling lonely." This practice fosters emotional safety by showing that anger often stems from outside triggers, not personal faults.

Elias and Gabe and more positive deposits

Day 7: Gabe, sensing the lingering tension about the HIV event, attempts a direct repair: "I know this event might be uncomfortable. What if we go only for an hour, then leave?" Elias admits he worries about running into acquaintances with questions he's not ready to answer. They compromise. Elias feels validated that Gabe isn't bulldozing him, while Gabe feels supported in his advocacy work. Their emotional bank sees a positive deposit.

Miguel defusing avoidance

Also Day 7: Miguel and Jude finally reserve 15 minutes to speak plainly about Jude's father's birthday. By tackling it head-on—despite the dread—Miguel steps out of stonewalling. The clarity of "Let's specifically talk about the father issue now" reduces the usual evasiveness. It's a small step, but that direct approach defuses months of avoidance.

Days 8–9: Intersectional tensions arise

Cyrus's racist microaggression episode

Day 8: At the office, Cyrus's coworkers laugh about "urban flamboyant styles," which is coded racism layered with homophobia. Furious, yet feeling powerless, Cyrus comes home. Jude, oblivious, mentions chores again. Cyrus snaps. Jude, noticing the mismatch, gently inquires if something else happened. Cyrus unloads about the racist subtext. Jude listens, acknowledges the significance, and offers empathy: "That's so invalidating. I'm sorry you faced that. Let's talk about how you feel." The conflict morphs into solidarity as Jude turns toward Cyrus's real hurt.

Elias and Gabe avoiding misread cues

Day 9: Elias's friend makes an ignorant remark: "Why date someone HIV-positive? That's complicated." Hurt and anxious, Elias withdraws from Gabe that night. Gabe senses stonewalling but calmly checks in: "You seem distant—did something happen?" Elias reveals the friend's comment. Gabe expresses support and reaffirms that external ignorance is not a reflection of their bond. By naming the root cause, they avoid a potential meltdown of misread cues.

Days 10–11: Proactive communication methods

Jude and Cyrus's emotional bids journal

Day 10: Jude and Cyrus read about an "emotional bids" journal in a self-help blog (or this book!). Deciding to do it for a few days, they record how often the other tries sharing something—like a sigh or story—and track each response. By Day 11, patterns emerge: Cyrus frequently half-listens if he's on his phone; Jude retreats if Cyrus seems uninterested. They vow to keep phones aside during shared meals, turning toward each other's remarks.

Elias and Gabe and the 30-minute "safe talk"

Also Day 10: After dinner, Elias and Gabe set 30 minutes for a "safe talk," focusing on unspoken feelings. Gabe confesses that he sometimes worries Elias might resent his activism. Elias clarifies it's not resentment; it's anxiety about being recognized at large gatherings. They talk it through gently, ending with a clearer understanding of each other's motives and fears.

Miguel's "conflict covenant"

Day 11: Miguel, longing to avoid abrupt stonewalling or topic shifts each time the father issues arise, writes a "conflict covenant" for himself:

> I won't dodge or abruptly change the topic when father's name comes up.
>
> I'll allow a short break if I feel panicked, but I'll come back to finish talking.
>
> I'll name my fear: I'm anxious he'll reject me again.

This personal code helps him navigate each new mention of father's birthday with honest communication, not reflexive evasion.

Days 12–13: External microaggressions and personal growth

Cyrus's ongoing struggle

Day 12: Another coworker insinuates flamboyance is unprofessional. Cyrus, outraged, returns home again. Jude, initiating talk about chores, triggers Cyrus's outburst: "Stop hassling me—I can't take it!" Quickly recognizing deeper pain, Jude says, "You seem really upset—did something at work happen?" Freed to express the real reason, Cyrus describes the second microaggression. Jude offers empathy, and they unite rather than argue. This time, chores fade into the background, overshadowed by Cyrus's legitimate frustration about coded racism and homophobia.

Elias and Gabe and a third-party issue

Day 13: Gabe's volunteer group invites Elias to speak about "Supporting HIV-positive partners." Elias panics, feeling unprepared. He snaps, "I told you, I'm not comfortable with that," brimming with defensiveness. They pause, do a mini-conflict debrief, discovering the triggers: Elias's fear of public attention vs. Gabe's desire for visible solidarity. They compromise: Elias might attend but remain offstage or only speak if he feels ready. This collaborative spirit avoids deeper negativity.

Miguel's progress

Miguel finally completes a heartfelt letter to Jude's father, explaining his love and the hope for a civil talk. Though anxious, he sees that direct honesty beats indefinite stonewalling. In this step, he reclaims agency, no longer letting fear dictate avoidance.

Day 14: Reflection and summation

Jude and Cyrus turning toward

Reviewing their "emotional bids" journal, they notice repeated slipups: Cyrus's phone usage during key moments and Jude's subsequent withdrawal. They commit to phone-free dinners each night, ensuring they both consistently turn toward each other's daily ups and downs.

Elias and Gabe, reducing negative cycles

Elias and Gabe attend part of the HIV-awareness event together. Elias, though uneasy, shows support by simply being there. Gabe feels seen and appreciated. That night, they talk it through calmly, each affirming that while they differ in comfort levels, mutual respect helps them navigate these external pressures. They've also significantly reduced negative cycles like contempt or stonewalling since practicing calmer dialogues.

Miguel's directness over indefinite silence

Miguel confides in Jude about sending the letter: "I'm terrified, but at least I'm not hiding anymore." Even if Jude's father's reply is negative, Miguel feels relief in choosing directness over indefinite silence. Their dynamic improves, too, since Jude sees Miguel taking courageous steps and admires him for it.

Through small, consistent actions—recognizing emotional bids, halting negative spirals, clarifying identity-based challenges—each participant in these scenarios experiences tangible improvements in their communication and emotional health.

Larger themes and long-term maintenance

Intersectionality in communication

The scenarios highlight how racism, HIV stigma, and family conservatism can magnify normal communication hurdles. If you are repeatedly confronted with prejudice, your baseline stress is elevated, making you more prone to reacting swiftly or feeling misunderstood. A key takeaway is to name these intersectional elements explicitly. Telling a partner, "I'm feeling singled out for being a gay man of color at work, so I'm extra-sensitive," fosters empathy. Similarly, if you're trans and anxious about being misgendered, letting your partner or friend know how that fear influences your daily mood can keep them from misinterpreting your withdrawal.

The ongoing nature of emotional bank deposits

We can't fill our emotional bank once and be done. This is an *everyday practice*. You might do a brilliant job responding to your partner's bids all week, then one stressful Friday leads to multiple missed bids, incurring emotional debt. Recognizing the cyclical nature helps us avoid complacency. The moment you sense tension, consider: "Have we missed a series of small bids lately? Are we 'overdrawn'?" Then intentionally add fresh deposits: a warm check-in, a sincere apology, or an empathetic hug.

Re-evaluating routines and rituals

Rituals form the backbone of stable communication. Over time, though, your life changes—new job, health issues, shifting social circles—so routines might need refreshing. Here are some ideas:

- *Semi-annual communication retreat:* Spend a weekend away from daily stress, phones off, dedicating blocks of time to discuss recurring issues, future goals, or personal growth.
- *Monthly check-in:* If you or your partner experience ongoing microaggressions or transphobia, a monthly talk about it fosters deeper understanding and solidarity.

Using professional or communal resources

If you find yourselves repeating the same negative cycles—stonewalling, contempt, or misreading each other's bids

—gay-affirming therapy or LGBTQ+ support groups can help. Even single men can benefit from refining conflict resolution and communication with a counselor or in group settings, reinforcing that seeking help is not an admission of failure but an investment in healthier bonds.

Conclusion: cultivating a lifelong dialogue

Communication is nuanced. It involves emotional readiness, past baggage, cultural scripts, even physiological stress. Dr. Gottman's research (Gottman and Silver 1999, 2015) supplies an empirical foundation, but each relationship also has unique quirks—maybe one partner is conflict-avoidant from a traumatic adolescence, or someone else is hyper-vigilant after a family's partial acceptance. If you're feeling overwhelmed, break it down:

- Try the "emotional bids" journal for a week.
- Then incorporate one structured "conflict debrief."
- Later, revisit the more in-depth sections or the extended case study scenarios for deeper insight.

Looking ahead

Chapters 8 and 9 will delve into *advanced conflict resolution* and *perpetual conflicts*, showing how these daily communication skills form the bedrock for tackling heavier issues (like finances, open relationships, or co-parenting). Chapter 10 then explores *forging a shared future or personal vision*, especially relevant if you're deciding how to integrate personal growth with a partner's evolving needs. The robust daily communication frameworks from this chapter ensure that you'll approach bigger decisions from a place of trust and mutual respect rather than reactionary stress.

Here are some extra ideas to sustain and deepen your communication practices long after you finish reading.

MINI-RETREAT FOR COMMUNICATION TUNE-UP

Purpose: To refresh and strengthen communication skills in a focused, distraction-free setting.

Time needed: Half-day to a weekend.

Who with: Partner, best friend, or chosen family member.

Plan the retreat. Choose a date, turn off devices, and select a quiet location.

"Four horsemen" review: Each person shares recent moments when they slipped into critique, contempt, defensiveness, or stonewalling, and how they might have used the antidote instead.

Emotional bids check: Compare notes on whether you turn toward each other's small signals or remarks.

Safe talk hour: Carve out a calm, uninterrupted hour to voice hidden anxieties or aspirations.

For singles: Try a shorter version with a close friend, focusing on how you each handle conflict or provide emotional support.

BREAKDOWN VS. BREAKTHROUGH

Purpose: To transform moments of contempt into opportunities for vulnerability and cooperation.

Time needed: 5–10 minutes in the moment.

Pause when you feel sarcasm, eye-rolling, or other contempt signals.

Ask yourself: "What's under this reaction? Am I afraid of not being heard?"

Replace contempt with vulnerability by stating the core feeling ("I feel worried about...").

Notice how the conversation shifts toward cooperation rather than attack.

DIGITAL DETOX

Purpose: To remove distractions and open more space for connection.

Time needed: One evening or a full weekend.

Commit to a set time with no phone or digital devices.

Be present for the small moments—comments, sighs, shared humor—that might otherwise go unnoticed.

Journal about how you felt and what emotional bids you observed.

Reflect on how removing distractions affected your closeness.

SINGLE MEN'S REFLECTIONS

Purpose: To build communication skills before entering a romantic relationship.

Time needed: Ongoing, practiced with friends and chosen family.

Identify moments when you can turn toward a friend's emotional bids.

Practice calmly discussing tensions without defensiveness.

Notice how empathy deepens your friendships over time.

Reflect on how these habits prepare you for future romantic partnerships.

If you're single, practicing these tools with your social circle ensures that when romance appears, you're already skilled at turning toward emotional bids or calmly discussing tensions. Good communication fosters every relationship, romantic or not. Over time, you'll see how genuine empathy in day-to-day friendships multiplies your overall sense of support and readiness for deeper connections.

AFFIRMATIONS AND POSITIVE SELF-TALK

Purpose: To reduce defensiveness and support healthy communication through self-compassion.

Time needed: 1–2 minutes before a challenging conversation.

Choose an affirmation such as:

"I deserve to be heard, and so does the other person."
"I can handle this calmly."

"It's okay to show my feelings."

Repeat it before and during the conversation.

Notice if it softens your tone, lowers tension, or makes vulnerability easier.

Reflect afterward on any shifts in connection.

Final encouragement

Communication is where everything you've learned about trauma, self-compassion, trust, and intimacy meets the real world—the very words that pass between you and another person. Each moment you choose empathy over dismissal, or gentleness over accusation, you're building a safer, kinder emotional ecosystem. Over weeks and months, these small interactions weave a tapestry of mutual understanding that no single grand gesture can replace.

If you find yourself stumbling—missing emotional bids, lashing out, or reverting to old defensive patterns—see it not as a final verdict but as a chance to refine. Revisit the relevant exercises, or reach out to a friend or therapist who "gets" the unique complexities of gay men's emotional landscapes. Step by step, you can repattern your communication habits, nurturing relationships that feel supportive, honest, and life-affirming. Whether you're single or partnered, younger or older, cis or trans, these daily communication skills stand as building blocks for the sense of belonging and authentic connection you genuinely deserve.

CHAPTER 8

Emotional Cartography

Discovering Your Partner's Inner World

Beyond everyday conversation

Communication is the backbone of any relationship, and for gay men—including gay trans men—facing particular social pressures or personal histories, our usual check-ins can leave a world of unspoken truths beneath the surface. Emotional cartography goes beyond the typical "How was your day?" chats to unearth the subtle emotional terrains that shape each other's fears, joys, insecurities, and core beliefs. Think of it as learning your partner's "emotional landmarks"—those unique places within them where identity, history, and vulnerability converge—so that you can love each other with deeper empathy and understanding.

Earlier, we explored foundational trust and basic communication skills. Here, we're diving one layer deeper. Emotional cartography moves us past everyday exchanges into the territory of honest self-revelation: the quiet stories or cultural pressures we carry, the childhood fears that linger, the parts of ourselves we've always kept safely tucked away. By bringing these hidden facets into the light, we create a bond that can weather tension, conflict, or outside judgment.

A deeper kind of understanding: the transformative power of mapping

Society can overlook or marginalize gay relationships, and gay trans men often face an extra layer of misunderstanding—even within parts of the LGBTQ+ community. Against that backdrop, having someone who truly "gets" you can be a potent source of healing. Emotional cartography offers a way to:

- *Heal old wounds:* Every time you share and receive compassion, you overwrite painful memories—like being rejected for who you are—with a fresh narrative of acceptance.
- *Strengthen long-term resilience:* These mapping moments help you build a well of empathy, so you can stand by each other through major life events—whether it's moving to a new city, facing family conflict, navigating job stresses, or dealing with complicated questions around identity.

Bringing emotional cartography into daily life

We're all used to daily or weekly check-ins—"How was your day?" or "Work go okay?" But a mapping moment goes further. It's a deliberate invitation to share parts of our emotional interior we normally keep locked away.

GUIDED CURIOSITY WALK

Purpose: To create space for deeper conversations in a relaxed, non-threatening setting.

Time needed: 20–40 minutes.

Choose a walking route—around the block, through a park, or anywhere comfortable.

Ask one thoughtful question, such as: "What's one thing you wish others understood about you but rarely get to say?"

Let the conversation flow naturally; avoid steering it too quickly.

End with a moment of appreciation for what you learned about each other.

If you're single: Invite a close friend or family member for the walk. Use the question to learn something new about each other's inner worlds, even if you've known each other for years.

If you're dating: Use the walk to move beyond surface-level dating talk and explore values, hopes, or vulnerabilities in a gentle way.

SHARED CREATIVE OUTLETS

Purpose: To use creativity as a bridge to emotional sharing when direct talk feels too vulnerable.

Time needed: 30–60 minutes.

Pick an activity—drawing, baking, making music, or choreographing a playful dance.

As you engage, notice the emotional tone between you.

When finished, gently ask:

"What feelings came up for you while we were doing that?"

Share your own reflections to invite mutual openness.

If you're single: Try the activity with a friend or even solo. Journal about what came up for you emotionally as you created, and consider sharing it with someone you trust.

If you're dating: Choose an activity that feels low-pressure and fun—something where laughter and play can naturally invite more openness.

RELAXED EVENING REFLECTION

Purpose: To foster deeper intimacy through intentional, distraction-free conversation.

Time needed: 15–30 minutes weekly.

Choose one evening a week to be your "mapping moment." Turn off devices, dim the lights, and get comfortable.

Each partner shares a single question or personal story.

Resist filling the silence—let pauses create space for thought and vulnerability.

If you're single: Call or video chat with a friend and use the same format—one question or personal story each.

If you're dating: Suggest this as a ritual to nurture connection early in the relationship, even if you don't live together.

ENCOURAGING MUTUAL VULNERABILITY

Purpose: To build trust and deepen connection by modeling openness.

Time needed: Integrated into any mapping moment.

After your partner shares, offer a parallel story from your own life—an old wound, hidden dream, or meaningful memory.

Acknowledge any fears you have about sharing, such as those related to body image, masculinity, or identity.

Reaffirm that you value their openness and feel safe together in this space.

If you're single: Practice by sharing something personal with a friend you trust, then note how they respond and how it feels to be vulnerable.

If you're dating: Lead with openness in small doses—sharing a personal insight or a gentle fear—so your date feels safe reciprocating.

Handling reluctance or resistance

Not everyone is ready to dive in at the same pace. Sometimes your partner may need more time before confronting deep issues. If so:

- *Check consent:* "I'd love to talk about something meaningful—are you up for that tonight?" This small courtesy respects your partner's emotional bandwidth.

- *Respect boundaries:* If they hesitate, respond gently: "I understand this might be tough. We can always try again later."
- *Start light:* Try a topic like favorite holiday traditions or childhood highlights before delving into darker corners like familial rejection or past trauma.

Overcoming emotional overload

Emotional cartography can stir up strong feelings, especially if you're revisiting past hurts. For gay trans men, certain memories—coming out moments, medical transition obstacles, dealing with misinformation—can carry an extra emotional charge. If this is the case:

- *Pause and ground:* If you sense anxiety spiking, try a grounding technique together: a few deep breaths, noticing the temperature of the room, or focusing on something comforting like a favorite cushion.
- *Offer reassurance:* "We don't need to solve every issue right now. I'm here for you, no rush." Affirming you're not pushing them helps keep trust intact.
- *Follow up:* After the conversation, maybe the next day, check in: "How did you feel about what we discussed?" This gently closes the loop so no leftover tension festers.

Taking time to map your own emotional landscape is just as vital. When you come to your partner with honesty about your scars (literal or metaphorical) and your own growth edges, you're showing them you want a relationship built on mutual courage.

WRITING A SUPPORTIVE LETTER TO YOUR YOUNGER SELF

Purpose

This exercise invites you to connect with your younger self, the child you once were, and offer him the words, compassion, and presence you might have longed for.

Why it matters: Many gay men grew up without models of love that felt safe or affirming. Writing to your younger self allows you to reclaim that inner relationship, to become the protective, nurturing figure you may have needed back then.

Find a quiet space. Take a breath. Maybe bring to mind a photo or memory of yourself at a younger age—7, 11, 15—any time when you felt unsure, scared, or unseen.

Write a letter to him from your current self. Let it come from the heart.

Use the prompts below to guide you, but feel free to go off-script:

- "I remember how you felt when..."
- "You didn't deserve to be treated like..."
- "If I could go back, I would tell you..."
- "Here's what I admire about you..."
- "You were never too much. You were..."
- "What you didn't know then was..."
- "One thing I wish someone had said to you is..."

For example:

Dear Little Me,

I remember how quiet you got when people teased you. How hard you tried to be good, to be small, to not get caught liking what you liked. I want you to know—you were never wrong.

Not for loving who you loved.
Not for crying when others didn't.
You were a boy full of tenderness. Of magic.

I see that now.

You don't have to hide anymore.
I'm here, and I won't leave.

Optional reflections:

- How did it feel to write this?
- What surprised you?
- What does that younger part of you still long to hear?

50+ questions for emotional cartography

Here is a curated list of questions to spark deeper dialogue. Use them sparingly—one or two at a time can unearth plenty. Grouped by theme, they're designed to help you and your partner find each other's emotional coordinates.

A. Past influences and family dynamics

- What's a childhood moment that still shapes how you see yourself today?

- Were emotions freely discussed in your family, or did everyone stay silent about deeper feelings?
- Is there a memory of feeling genuinely accepted—or harshly rejected—for being gay or trans?
- Who in your family most influenced your self-esteem, for better or worse?
- How do you feel those early lessons still play out in our relationship?

Additional questions for gay trans men

- Did you have any support from family or friends during your transition, or did you navigate it mostly alone?
- How did your parents or guardians talk about gender, if at all, when you were growing up?
- What do you wish you could tell your younger self about living as a trans man?

B. Present feelings and challenges

- Which daily stress feels heaviest on your shoulders right now, and how could I help ease it?
- When do you feel your calmest and most at peace? Can we build more moments like that into our routine?
- Is there a new habit or ritual we could adopt that would help you feel more grounded?
- Does your work or social life spill over into our time together? How can we handle that gracefully?

- In the face of negativity from the outside world, what coping strategies do you rely on?

Additional questions for gay trans men

- How does navigating trans-specific healthcare or documentation affect your day-to-day well-being?
- Is there any support (emotional, logistical) that would make your present challenges feel less daunting?

C. Hidden hopes and insecurities

- What ambition or dream have you been hesitant to share with me?
- Which insecurities—about your looks, intelligence, or skills—do you keep mostly hidden?
- When you imagine your best self, what core qualities shine through?
- What do you think I could do to help you see that positive version of yourself more often?
- Are there any specific labels or identity terms that feel affirming (or not) for you right now?

Additional questions for gay trans men

- If you experience dysphoria, how can I best support you—physically, emotionally, or with language?
- What aspects of being trans bring you unexpected joy or pride?

D. Relationship dynamics and connection

- How do you picture us growing together in the next few years?
- What's one recurring misunderstanding we have, and how might we heal it?
- Which moments make you feel truly heard in our arguments or heavier discussions?
- What small differences between us do you secretly cherish—even if they annoy you sometimes?
- In what ways can we make our daily interactions more intentional and less autopilot?

Additional question for gay trans men

- Does anything about our relationship dynamic feel shaped by assumptions about cis vs. trans roles? How can we talk about that openly?

E. Future visions and shared projects

- What's a travel or adventure goal you'd love us to share?
- How do you feel about starting or expanding a family, whether that's children, pets, or a broader chosen family?
- If resources were unlimited, how would you like us to make a difference—through activism, creativity, community support?
- What sort of lifestyle do you envision in the long run—urban loft, quiet countryside, globe-trotting?

- Where do you see our relationship in 10 years, and what might help us get there?

Additional question for gay trans men

- Do you have any dreams about community-building or advocacy in trans spaces that you'd love to share with me?

F. External pressures and societal stress

- In what ways do societal judgments or stereotypes still affect your sense of self?
- When you face homophobia or transphobia, what's the most supportive thing I can do?
- How do you feel about public displays of affection, and what shaped that comfort level?
- Do you feel you can be open at work or around extended family, or do you need to mask certain parts of yourself?
- If you had one message for straight society about gay or trans relationships, what would it be?

G. Vulnerabilities and healing

- What's an old wound—maybe from a past relationship or family dynamic—that still hurts?
- Do you fear abandonment, and if so, what kind of reassurance helps you feel safer?

- When you're overwhelmed, do you prefer space, comforting touch, or gentle questions?
- Is there a side of you I haven't fully seen yet?
- What regret do you hold, and how can I best support your healing?

Additional question for gay trans men

- If you are trans, has any part of your transition journey (medical, social, legal) left an emotional scar you still want to process?
- What has been your most affirming or healing experience as a trans man, and how can I honor that milestone with you?

H. Celebrations and identity

- Which aspects of being gay or trans feel affirming, joyful, or just plain fun?
- What's a personal achievement—big or small—you're proud of right now, and why does it matter to you?
- Which traditions—cultural, religious, or community-based—bring you a sense of belonging?
- Who inspired you to accept yourself—maybe a mentor, a public figure, or a friend?
- What's something about our relationship that feels distinctly ours, something that stands apart from any other bond?

I. Family, friends, and social circles

- How do you view our chosen family or close friend group? Anything you'd like to see shift or grow?
- Which of your family members would you like me to understand better, and how can I try?
- Are there any traditions (yours or mine) we could reinvent or blend to feel more aligned with who we are now?
- How do you hope our families—whether biological, chosen, or a mix—might evolve in their acceptance of us?
- Is there a close friend who shapes your views on relationships or identity?

J. Relationship growth and appreciation

- When did you feel most cared for by me recently, even if it was a small gesture?
- What's one conflict we handled gracefully, and what can we learn from that?
- What is a habit of mine that you appreciate more than I realize?
- How do you feel about our communication now compared to when we first started dating?
- If our love was a movie soundtrack, what emotional theme might play?

Strategies and scripts for handling resistance

Even with these questions in hand, some partners might resist going deep—due to past traumas, fear of judgment, or internalized messages telling them it's "too much." Here are some scripts you might like to use.

For a gentle approach

> This topic feels vulnerable, and I appreciate anything you're comfortable sharing. If this isn't a good moment, we can circle back.

For offering reassurance

> I'm not trying to fix you. I want to understand what you've been through so we can navigate it together.

For managing emotional overload

If either of you becomes tearful or tense, pause:

> Let's take a break—maybe breathe or get some fresh air. We don't have to solve everything tonight.

For self-reflection

Emotional cartography flows both ways. If your partner's story triggers something in you—maybe an old jealousy, an unresolved fear—take a note of it and share that realization if it feels right. You both have emotional terrains to map.

Encouraging cultural sensitivity

Not all gay men, including trans men, share the same cultural or religious background. Some grew up in environments where emotions were never discussed; others learned to wear their hearts on their sleeves.

Validate different expressions

A partner who grew up in a family that discouraged deep emotional talk may need extra time to open up. Let them move at their own pace.

Stay curious

Ask, "How did your family or culture handle emotional issues? Were they big on open sharing, or did they keep things private?" Understanding their norms helps you adapt how you approach sensitive topics.

PRACTICING EMOTIONAL CARTOGRAPHY

Aaron (forties, cis gay man) and Nathan (forties, cis gay man) had been dating for a few months. Aaron felt Nathan rarely opened up about deeper feelings. Instead of pushing, Aaron first opened up about a heartbreak that left him feeling "too emotional." Seeing that honesty, Nathan admitted he'd been shamed by a sibling whenever he cried, labeled as "weak." They then used just a couple of questions from the "Past influences" section—talking about early messages around masculinity—and discovered how shame from childhood still weighed on them.

Outcome

They started pausing during arguments to ask, "Is this triggering that old feeling of being weak?" Over time, the arguments became more supportive conversations. Nathan later said, "I never knew it could feel *good* to be emotional, like there's space for it without ridicule."

One step closer to a more intimate bond

Emotional cartography isn't about suddenly mastering your partner's entire history; it's a thoughtful unveiling, a chance to replace surface-level chats with honest glimpses into each other's hearts. Each time you respond with kindness to a vulnerable admission, each time you share something tender about yourself, you're building a foundation that can endure external judgments, your own insecurities, and the everyday stressors of life.

Call to action

- *Choose one or two questions:* Don't feel compelled to tackle too many questions at once. The goal is depth, not an emotional marathon.
- *Set a "mapping moment:"* Pick a relaxed time—a Sunday morning with coffee, a scenic drive, or a quiet evening—to gently bring up your chosen questions.
- *Celebrate small discoveries:* Did you learn why your partner avoids a certain holiday or lights up at a specific type of music? Acknowledge it: "Thanks for sharing that—I never knew it mattered so much to you."

- *Reflect on your own map:* After your partner shares, open up about your own experiences. Reciprocity builds trust.

Final reflection prompt: Think of a recurring misunderstanding in your relationship. How might it ease if you understood your partner's deeper history or raw feelings about it? Which one or two questions from this chapter could help you both shed fresh light on that cycle?

Closing encouragement: Whatever your answer, remember that even the smallest step, asking a single question with real curiosity, pausing instead of rushing to "fix," or offering a tender piece of your own backstory, can transform day-to-day conversation into a powerful act of love. Over time, emotional cartography becomes a treasured practice, guiding you through each other's inner worlds. In a culture that often demands quick answers or polished fronts, you and your partner can choose to truly see and be seen, no filters, no masks, just genuine presence and acceptance.

CHAPTER 9

Navigating Perpetual Conflicts

Beyond the Thorny Undergrowth

When the same disagreement won't disappear

Have you ever noticed yourself and your partner cycling through the same argument over and over? Maybe it starts with a mundane issue—like how to manage finances or how often to see friends—but it quickly spirals into something bigger. If you're a gay man, you might already shoulder the weight of societal bias or family rejection, so these endless debates can feel especially draining. Yet the most persistent conflicts, the ones tied to core values or personality traits, can also become doorways to deeper empathy and growth—if we handle them well.

This chapter goes beyond everyday communication tips, focusing on the *unsolvable* or *perpetual conflicts* that reflect central parts of your identity. Think of differing comfort levels with family visits, contrasting views on how "out" to be in public, or deeply rooted disagreements about spending vs. saving money. By learning specific frameworks—like conflict covenants, conflict debriefs, and shared understanding—you can coexist lovingly with these differences, rather than trying in vain to make them vanish.

Defining perpetual conflicts and why they matter

A perpetual conflict arises from fundamental differences in upbringing, personality, or worldview. These are *not* minor misunderstandings over who forgot to buy milk. Instead, they revolve around the deeper aspects of who you and your partner are—like cherished cultural norms, spiritual beliefs, or personal comfort zones formed by past experiences. Because they tap into your sense of self, neither partner can simply "fix" or "change" the underlying root.

Why this tension can feel heavier for gay men

For gay men, repeated internal conflicts add to external pressures: microaggressions, possible family disapproval, or a community that might have expectations about how relationships "should" work. If you grew up hiding parts of yourself or constantly validating your worth, a fundamental clash with your partner might feel especially threatening—*another sign you're not accepted.* But these recurring disagreements are normal in all relationships. The key is learning to approach them with empathy, humor, and proven strategies, rather than seeing them as a sign of failure.

Perpetual vs. solvable conflicts

- *Perpetual conflicts:* Core personality traits or life visions. No matter how you talk about them, the essence of the conflict remains.

- *Solvable conflicts:* Specific tasks or short-term solutions, like coordinating grocery shopping.

When you recognize that some conflicts simply *won't* disappear, it becomes possible to handle them lovingly. Acceptance doesn't mean surrender; it means transforming what could be destructive into an ongoing dialogue shaped by respect.

Looking deeper: connections to deeper identity or past trauma

How personal history fuels recurring clashes

For many gay men, the experiences of growing up in unwelcoming environments or facing hostility can create triggers around acceptance, belonging, or autonomy. This background can quietly power a conflict. For example, if you once felt stifled at home, you might now crave a wide social circle and spontaneous events, while your partner, who felt insecure about finances, needs careful planning and predictability.

Intersections with family, race, or other identities

If you or your partner are men of color, immigrants, trans, disabled, or from a strict religious family, each repeated conflict can be laced with extra emotional layers. You might fear your partner's approach invalidates your cultural identity or your sense of safety. Recognizing those layers helps both partners approach the conflict with humility, realizing it's not *just* about chores or vacations but about deeper identity or survival themes.

Have you ever felt your heart race when your partner challenges a practice you hold dear, because it's tied to your culture or earliest sense of self-worth? This is why repeated arguments can sting so intensely—and why empathy is paramount.

Core strategies for perpetual conflicts

Here are four major methods for living peacefully with repeated disagreements that stem from core differences. Each strategy includes bridging notes on how it addresses the deeper complexities unique to gay men's experiences.

Conflict covenant

A conflict covenant is a joint agreement on how to handle hot-button issues. It sets rules—like no name-calling, a code word for breaks, or a vow to validate each other's perspective. By formalizing these guidelines, you ensure that even repeated arguments stay within respectful boundaries.

Steps to make it happen

- *Name the core tension:* "We differ on public displays of affection."
- *Outline basic courtesy:* "No mocking remarks like 'You're such a wimp for not wanting to hold hands in public.'"
- *Include a safe word:* If tension escalates, one partner can say "Pause" or another chosen word to get a 5-minute cooldown.
- *Reassure each other:* "We both want closeness, even if we approach it differently."

Bridging back to recurring issues

For gay men, sensitivity to public scrutiny can add another

layer of pressure to recurring disagreements. A predetermined "no shaming, no insulting" rule helps prevent these moments from spiraling into personal attacks or reactivating old homophobic traumas. Each time the conflict flares, the Covenant serves as a steady reminder: "We might never fully solve this, but we agree to treat each other kindly regardless." Over time, this shared commitment shifts the focus from "winning" an argument to preserving respect and safety, even in the heat of disagreement.

Conflict debrief

A conflict debrief is a post-argument review. Rather than forgetting the fight once emotions subside, you reflect together on what triggered each reaction, how you felt physically (like a tightness in your chest or sweaty palms), and which deeper fears or insecurities surfaced.

Steps to conduct a conflict debrief

- *Pinpoint the latest recurrence:* "We argued over me wanting to attend a gay networking event alone vs. you feeling left out."
- *Dig deeper:* Each partner describes their perspective. Perhaps one is worried about being replaced, while the other fears being smothered.
- *Commit to minor tweaks:* Maybe you text each other once or twice during solo outings, bridging the anxiety about feeling excluded.
- *End on a positive note:* A compliment or a quick hug affirms that, while the conflict remains, the bond endures.

Bridging back to recurring issues

By dissecting each recurrence calmly, you glean insight into the patterns fueling the tension. Over multiple debriefs, you unearth the emotional "landmarks" of your unsolvable conflict. Each new argument becomes less volatile because you already know the triggers, making it simpler to navigate next time. For gay men, it's a relief to realize the friction is less about "I'm unworthy" or "You don't love me" and more about old triggers meeting real-time stress.

Shared understanding framework

In a shared understanding approach, each partner explains *why* a stance is significant. For instance, if one partner wants closeness to an extended family that once displayed borderline homophobia, it might be rooted in cultural or personal identity. The other partner might be perplexed, but hearing the emotional backstory fosters empathy.

Steps for shared understanding

- *Outline each core need:* "I need to maintain family ties because it's part of my personal identity."
- *Identify the nonnegotiables:* "I won't hide that you're my partner, even if they disapprove."
- *Craft a "We" statement:* "We'll attend certain family events together, openly, but skip those that might be overtly hostile."

Bridging back to perpetual conflicts

A shared understanding helps you move away from seeing each

other's stances as purely inconvenient or irrational. Instead, you see them as integral facets of your partner's history or cultural positioning. Even though the conflict remains—like deciding how often to visit conservative relatives—*both* of you feel more validated, leading to fewer hurt feelings when the disagreement arises again.

Finding the deeper story

By asking "Why is that so upsetting?" multiple times, you peel back layers of old trauma, insecurities, or cultural norms that shape your partner's stance. This is different from a quick solution hunt; it's a deep dive into each other's emotional archives.

Sample walkthrough

- *Start with the present issue:* "You always get anxious when we talk about adopting a child."
- *Ask why:* "Why does it bother you so much?"
- *Listen:* Maybe your partner shares a memory of being told gay men shouldn't raise children or fear they'd replicate an abusive parenting style.
- *Validate:* "I see how that old messaging is fueling your hesitation now."
- *Collaborate:* Could you speak with affirming families who are gay parents? Reassure each other about seeking supportive communities?

How this ties to ongoing conflict

Even if adopting remains a point of tension, repeatedly

unearthing these deeper layers shifts the conversation from "You're just stalling!" to "I understand your fear is real and based on hurtful experiences or personal doubts." The conflict might still surface with each mention of parenthood, but the empathy gained fosters patience and emotional closeness.

Emotional safety and humor: finding the right mix

Building emotional safety over time

Perpetual disagreements can either corrode or fortify your sense of safety, depending on how you handle them. Each time your partner expresses vulnerability ("I'm terrified of public displays of affection because I was once attacked for looking 'too gay'"), your empathetic listening deposits trust in your emotional bank. Over months or years, this bank ensures repeated arguments don't become existential threats.

The role of humor

We've all had those moments where everything feels so heavy that a tiny bit of humor can break the tension. For unsolvable issues, a gentle comedic label—like "The great budget battle of 2023"—can remind you that you're on the same team, facing the conflict together. Just remember:

- Laugh at the situation, not your partner.
- Return to seriousness when addressing actual fears or trauma.

A quick laugh can help both of you breathe easier, then circle back to the real conversation with lowered defenses.

SASHA AND MIGUEL

Conflict at a glance

Sasha (forties, cis gay man) loves spontaneity due to a once-rigid childhood, while Miguel (forties, cis gay man) craves predictability after years of feeling invisible. They clash over weekend plans weekly.

Sensory details

Saturday morning: Sasha's eyes sparkle as he runs into the living room, phone in hand. "There's a last-minute Pride-themed brunch—let's go!" Miguel feels his stomach tighten. "I was counting on a quiet morning. Couldn't you have told me earlier?" Sasha tries a small grin. "Sorry—just saw the invite. We can do something else if you want."

Strategy implementation

- Conflict covenant: No calling each other "control freak" or "impulsive."
- Shared understanding: Sasha sees spontaneity as a form of freedom; Miguel needs mental prep.

Outcome

They still debate weekend plans, but each time they do, they refer to their rules and show a bit more humor, calling it "The Saturday surprise saga." Over time, the tension dips significantly.

AMIR AND JOSE

Conflict at a glance

Amir (thirties, cis gay man) wants jam-packed vacations, worried about "wasting life." José (thirties, cis gay man) craves unstructured rest, remembering an overbearing family dynamic.

Sensory details

Arriving at a European Airbnb. Amir's heart thumps with excitement: "We can do a full-day city tour tomorrow, then a wine bar at night!" José's neck tenses. "Could we have at least an afternoon to just wander without a plan?"

Strategy implementation:

- Conflict debrief after each meltdown: They realize the deeper story—Amir's fear of missing out, José's dread of being overwhelmed.
- Humor emerges: "No mega itinerary is complete without José's 'Chill time.'"

Outcome

The same conflict resurfaces each trip, but rarely escalates into hurtful fights. They talk calmly, acknowledging each other's triggers and forging partial solutions each time.

CAM AND LEON

Conflict at a glance

Cam is in his twenties and is a cis gay man. Cam's devout, collectivist family expects him to attend many events. Leon (twenties, trans gay man), from a more individualistic background, feels drained and sometimes unaccepted by Cam's relatives.

Sensory details

Sunday morning phone call: Cam's voice quivers. "My cousin's baby shower is today—she wants both of us there." Leon exhales sharply, chest tight. "Another day lost to feeling judged." Cam's eyes fill with quiet desperation. "I can't skip it, but I don't want you to be miserable."

Strategy implementation

- Conflict covenant: No guilt-tripping or "You're so selfish" statements.
- Finding the deeper story: Cam's loyalty is shaped by upbringing. Leon's frustration stems from repeated negative experiences at these gatherings.

Outcome

While the tension about extended family remains, each instance triggers less negativity. Leon sometimes joins in, sometimes not, but no longer sees Cam's stance as betrayal. They handle each new event with a little more calm, forging partial compromises that adapt over time.

The lifecycle of a perpetual conflict

Early stage: alarm bells

In a newer relationship, discovering a fundamental clash can feel like a deal-breaker. "Are we too incompatible?" or "Will this confirm the stereotype that gay men's relationships are unstable?" By naming the conflict as a deeper difference, you can shift from panic to exploration.

Middle stage: building systems

In the mid-stage, you refine strategies like conflict debriefs or covenants. You also test out comedic labeling or safe words, discovering what keeps arguments from exploding. You might see partial successes, with fewer blowups and a sense of *We can handle this*.

Long-term: established routines

Eventually, the conflict no longer rattles the foundation of your relationship. The repeated tension might remain—like city living vs. countryside—but you handle it with an ease that once seemed impossible. What started as a dreaded flashpoint becomes a recurring quirk of your dynamic, occasionally prompting grumbles or jokes, but seldom deep wounds.

Tracking and celebrating progress: why acknowledgment is crucial

Perpetual conflicts are, by definition, endless. Recognizing each small success or compromise is essential to stay motivated. You might keep a short journal, or, once a month, you might reflect: *Did we manage that old argument more kindly this time?*

Here are some examples of micro-victories:

- Pausing a heated argument for a calm breath instead of storming off.
- Ending on a warm note: "We still disagree, but I love you."

- Spotting humor—"There goes that 'city vs. suburbs' debate again"—before it spirals into anger.

When you see the repeated conflict as part of your story together, rather than a sign of failure each improvement feels like a genuine triumph. Over time, these micro-victories form a narrative of resilience.

Adapting over time

Rechecking conflict covenants, debriefs, and shared understanding

Whenever circumstances shift—maybe a career move, adopting children, or relocating—some pieces of your approach may need updating. The job that once fed your anxieties might be replaced by a calmer role, or a newly pressing family health issue might intensify debates about traveling for holidays.

Evolving identity and healing

If therapy or self-growth changes your triggers, the nature of the perpetual conflict can also shift. A partner who once panicked about saving money might gain confidence after a promotion, easing the tension around spending. The underlying conflict remains (like philosophical differences on how to use money), but the emotional load reduces as old wounds recede.

Thriving with the thorns still intact

Accepting that some conflicts remain

When two gay men build a life together, each brings unique

perspectives shaped by culture, childhood, and orientation. Some differences will never fully dissolve. Yet you can hold those differences gently, transforming friction into repeated chances to reaffirm your bond.

Transforming the meaning

Every time the same conflict reappears, it's not a sign of doom but that you're *still* two distinct individuals. You might say, "Yes, we're back here, but remember how we handled it better last time?" That phrase captures the essence: each iteration of the conflict can highlight your evolving empathy and creativity.

Here are some pitfalls to avoid:

- *Ignoring intersectional factors:* Overlooking how race, class, faith, or disability might complicate repeated conflicts is a recipe for misunderstanding.
- *Expecting a final resolution:* Hoping one big conversation will end a fundamental difference invites disappointment.
- *Neglecting self-care:* Repeated conflicts can be draining; ensure you have supportive friends, a therapist, or personal reflective space to process ongoing stress.

Putting these methods into practice

- *Name one perpetual conflict:* Choose the one conflict that drains you the most.
- *Pick one strategy:* Maybe establish a conflict covenant if you're prone to nasty fights, or a shared understanding framework if you suspect deeper cultural or personal roots.

- *Track small wins:* Over two or three flare-ups, watch for times you ended calmer or found partial compromises.
- *Adapt if needed:* If a chosen method doesn't help or feels stale, pivot to another (conflict debrief, finding the deeper story, or a brand-new approach).
- *Celebrate growth:* Acknowledge it's an ongoing process. Even modest improvements are meaningful.

Reflection prompt: Think about the last time you fought over that *same* persistent issue. What if you introduced a new approach—like stepping away for 5 minutes, or calmly asking "What deeper fear is fueling this?" How might that transform the moment from a draining spiral into a small step forward?

Conclusion: beyond the thorns

Perpetual conflicts can feel like the thorns on a rose: they're not going anywhere, yet they're surrounded by beauty and depth. Repeated debates, especially for gay men who might be juggling external prejudices, can sometimes overshadow love if left unmanaged. But armed with strategies like conflict covenants, debriefs, and deeper empathy, each recurring clash becomes a chance to say, "Yes, we differ. And we'll keep choosing each other regardless."

When you truly accept that not all disputes have a neat resolution—*and that's okay*—you create space for humor, hope, and mutual respect. Every repeated argument is one more opportunity to show that your bond transcends perfect agreement. Instead, it's rooted in a willingness to keep growing, keep showing compassion, and keep nurturing the shared life you've built, even when you see the world through different lenses.

CHAPTER 10

Moving Forward Together

Crafting Your Shared Future

Standing in the clearing of the forest

A vision of arrival and new beginnings

Picture yourself on a forest trail you've been walking for weeks or even months. Each bend has revealed a new part of your emotional world—old wounds, shifting self-beliefs, and moments of deeper trust in your relationships. Throughout this book, you've journeyed from uncovering trauma's roots to practicing self-compassion, from mapping attachment patterns to building intimate bonds, and from tackling daily disagreements to addressing persistent conflicts that never fully vanish. Now you stand in a tranquil clearing, the canopy above filtering gentle beams of light. This clearing is your place of rest and reflection, where you can appreciate how far you've come—and glimpse the road still ahead.

As you pause here, notice how each step has helped you loosen the grip of old burdens—internalized homophobia, transphobia, rejection fears, or the everyday stress of living in a world that isn't always welcoming. Maybe you're a trans gay man, once overwhelmed by dysphoria or worries about "passing," who's discovered new ways to see your body with compassion. Perhaps conflicts that once felt endless now seem solvable, or even hold unexpected insights. This final chapter invites you to celebrate your progress and plan the next leg of your journey, armed with greater emotional clarity and confidence.

Embracing the complexity of gay men's relationships

Whether you're a cis gay man or a trans gay man, forming healthy, enduring connections can feel like an uphill climb—due to prejudice, harmful clichés, family struggles, or other intersectional realities. Yet these same challenges can nurture a powerful mix of empathy and resilience. In this closing chapter, we'll gather the key themes from earlier chapters and imagine how they can bloom in your daily life. Ultimately, I encourage you to share what you've learned with others, building a supportive network where these lessons can flourish long after you turn the last page.

Here are some quick reflections on the lessons so far:

- Early chapters: You uncovered how trauma and cultural biases shape emotional triggers, self-worth, and attachment styles, especially within gay men's lives—and for some, layered with the unique experience of being a trans man.
- Midway: You embraced self-compassion as a foundation for healing old wounds, deepening intimacy, and navigating recurring relationship tensions.
- Later chapters: You discovered structured tools—like

conflict covenants and emotional cartography—that invite meaningful, growth-focused dialogue.

These ideas form a toolkit for the varied realities of gay men's relationships. Your mission now is to keep these tools alive and flexible, adapting them to each new insight or challenge.

Why it matters: It's easy to latch on to a single method that resonates most, but each piece of your journey supports the others. For instance, a stronger self-compassion practice amplifies your courage to be open in moments of intimacy, which in turn helps you face conflicts more calmly. If you're a trans gay man, the empathy you've built around your body and identity can make it easier to share concerns with a partner about your changing feelings or triggers. The more you nurture yourself, the more space you create for your partner, turning everyday disagreements into opportunities for greater understanding.

Celebrating growth: recognizing your own progress

Small shifts, profound changes

Transformation often surfaces in the little moments: you pause before saying something hurtful, breathe instead of running away, or speak aloud a fear you once kept hidden. Over time, these gestures add up. Maybe you and a partner no longer spiral into destructive arguments, or, if you're trans, you're more comfortable with top surgery scars and hormone changes. Or you may finally see yourself as truly worthy of love, rather than feeling you must "earn" closeness. Each tiny step signals how much you've grown.

The power of written reflection

If you haven't tried already, you might keep a simple diary of victories—like "I took a moment to breathe when I felt triggered." Reading over your entries down the line can help you see how you've evolved. For trans men, logging positive body experiences—like noticing less dysphoria or finding the right words to describe your transition—can be especially uplifting. These notes remind you just how resilient you are, even when life feels stuck.

> Which practice—self-compassion breaks, assertive communication, or something else—feels like your anchor when stress hits?

By briefly considering (or jotting down) your answer, you're more prepared to lean on it when the next challenge comes along.

Building a future-proof foundation: returning to key tools

Life unfolds in waves. New experiences arise, old traumas can resurface, and sometimes your sense of self or your relationship dynamic shifts—especially if you're navigating transitions as a trans man. Revisiting and refining your strategies helps you adapt to whatever comes your way, be it a personal crisis, a changing job, or unexpected developments in your transition. Each tool you've learned remains part of a living journey, not a static checklist.

Here's a quick reminder of the core frameworks:

- *Conflict covenants:* Jointly agreed-upon guidelines for

respectful conflict, along with a "safe word" to halt destructive spirals.

- *Self-compassion exercises:* Simple mantras or grounding techniques that soften shame and anxiety.
- *Emotional check-ins:* Consistent mini-conversations that keep misunderstandings from escalating.
- *Emotional cartography:* Gradual, curiosity-driven ways to reveal deeper life stories—bridging differences in body experiences or personal histories.

When setbacks occur—maybe you miss a partner's emotional bid or feel triggered by dysphoria—recognize it calmly and return to these frameworks. It's not a failure, just part of ongoing growth.

Balancing individual autonomy and shared dreams

Recognizing individual growth as ongoing

This book has zeroed in on relationships, yet your relationship with yourself matters most. If you discover a new interest or a new expression of your gender identity, embrace it. Encourage your partner to follow their spark, too. As you both evolve personally, your combined pool of insights and experiences deepens. If you're trans, feeling more secure in your body may lead to fresh excitement in your shared life, and the mutual sharing of these developments can revitalize your connection.

Joint goals that align with your values

Many couples find joy in shared projects, whether that's mentoring younger gay or trans men, volunteering at local LGBTQ+ centers, or planning to build a family—through adoption, fostering, or building a close-knit chosen family. Aligning on a vision underscores why you chose to walk this path together. Every milestone (like raising funds for a community program) reaffirms the power of your partnership.

> When did you, as a couple, last update your dreams for the future?

Asking open-ended questions fosters collaboration, revealing how your new goals might harmonize or spark further growth.

Engaging a larger community and intersectionality

Passing the torch

The lessons you've gathered—on managing trauma, dealing with recurring arguments, and employing self-compassion—can lift others who feel alone. By forming or joining a small support group for gay men (including trans men), or by hosting a casual workshop, you strengthen your own understanding and make a difference for others in need of guidance. Teaching someone else helps you embody these lessons more deeply.

Affirming identities across intersections

If you're a trans man, an older gay man, a gay man of color, or living with HIV, your unique experiences carry a special importance for those who share that journey. Speaking about your path—whether at a local center, online, or in small circles—can challenge misconceptions both inside and outside the gay community. You benefit as well, building a sense of shared resilience and camaraderie.

A broader impact

By living and sharing this process rooted in honesty and empathy, you help transform the narrative of what it means to be a gay man. Each person who sees real-life examples of healing, growth, and inclusive love can be motivated to question old stereotypes and open up new possibilities. In that way, you contribute to a broader cultural change, one conversation at a time.

Revisiting lessons in the face of life's surprises

The nature of unexpected twists

Change is a given. A health concern, an unplanned career turn, or new phases of your transition can disrupt the calm. Instead of seeing these as failures, you can treat them as opportunities to apply your well-honed tools—conflict debriefs, self-compassion, honest check-ins. The unpredictability of life doesn't have to unravel your progress; it can reinforce it.

RELOCATION CROSSROADS

Purpose: To navigate major life changes—like a potential move—while staying grounded in empathy and clarity.

Time needed: 30–60 minutes.

Clarify desires: Each partner names their deeper pull—whether it's excitement for a fresh start, fear of losing community, or a mix of both.

Offer self-compassion: Remind each other that fear, hesitation, or mixed feelings are normal and not a sign of ingratitude.

Conflict debrief: After each discussion, reflect together on what emotional undercurrents surfaced—such as fear of isolation, longing for stability, or hunger for change.

Map possibilities: Discuss potential scenarios (stay, move, try long distance) without rushing to decide. Keep the focus on mutual understanding rather than winning the argument.

If you're single: Use this exercise to explore your own mixed feelings about a big move. Journaling or talking it out with a trusted friend can help clarify which fears and hopes feel most important to honor.

If you're dating: Use this framework early in the conversation to prevent defensiveness. The goal is not to make a quick decision but to ensure each partner feels heard, understood, and respected as you explore options.

Ongoing tune-ups

Think about having a "relationship check-up" every three to six months—or whenever big changes appear. Ask: *Are there new stresses we haven't addressed? Are we still practicing the tools we found helpful?* This gentle routine keeps you alert and flexible as life evolves.

> Which approach—conflict covenants, self-compassion mantras, or something else—will you rely on next time life throws you a curveball?

Letting yourself answer that question, even briefly, can ground you, reminding you that you're far from helpless when challenges arise.

Final words of encouragement

Recognizing how far you've come

Across these chapters, you've dared to face shadows once overshadowed by shame or fear. You've looked at family dynamics, confronted internalized homophobia or transphobia, and questioned whether you truly deserve love. You've practiced naming your needs—maybe for the first time—and discovered how freeing it is to receive acceptance instead of judgment. If you're a trans gay man, you may have explored new layers of bodily comfort, finding fresh ways to be both desirable and at peace in your own skin. Those steps are no small feat; they reveal a remarkable capacity to adapt and thrive.

A journey of ongoing discovery

Though this chapter signals the end of the book, your learning continues. You'll meet fresh joys and fresh complications. Sometimes you'll regress—perhaps ignoring a partner's emotional hint or snapping without thinking. Yet each slip can be a teacher, nudging you to lean again on your toolbox: self-compassion, mindful communication, or conflict resolution.

Real transformation welcomes imperfection, as long as you keep growing and returning to empathy.

A personal thank you and a forward look

Writing this and reflecting on how cis gay men and trans gay men navigate relationships wasn't about offering a quick fix—it was about showing that empathy, humor, and concrete tools can make our lives so much richer. Thank you for allowing this book to be part of your journey. Your willingness to grapple with vulnerability and conflict shows a courage that defines real growth and lasting love.

Stepping forward together

Parting vision

Visualize yourself once more in that clearing, the forest around you both familiar and still full of surprises. You're armed with techniques for communication, self-kindness, and trans-inclusive acceptance if that's part of your story. In every moment—be it playful or challenging—you have the power to nurture genuine closeness, fueled not by a quest for perfection but by a desire to understand and be understood. Each step forward is a chance to reaffirm your own worth and that of the people who walk beside you.

Enacting community change

If you feel moved to share your progress, consider hosting a small gathering at a local LGBTQ+ center or posting a note on social media about how mindful discussions or gentle conflict resolution have shaped your dating or relationship life. If you're a trans man, your personal story might shine a light for someone uncertain about where they belong. Through such acts, you transform your individual journey into communal growth. Others who feel trapped or unseen may find the impetus to start their own healing process.

Continuing the legacy of compassion

By caring for yourself with tenderness, meeting your partner's needs with openness, and honoring the reality that both of you are still evolving, you keep this book's legacy alive. Even if your relationship shifts form or you enter a new life phase, the lessons of honest communication and inclusive love remain guiding lights.

Close your eyes for a moment. Reflect on the trail you've already braved—moments of confusion, tears, laughter, and genuine breakthroughs—and the horizon that stretches onward. Each careful step, each reaffirmation of your identity and capacity to love, shapes a story that goes far beyond these pages. Keep walking, keep learning, and keep telling yourself the truth that you are profoundly worthy of real connection and joy.

Resources and Support

A note from the author

In this book, we've traversed personal histories, explored painful echoes of trauma, nurtured self-compassion, and delved into the nuances of building trust and intimacy. But healing and growth rarely unfold in isolation. Sometimes you need a friendly voice, a local support group, or even a legal advocate. Here, you'll find a curated list of organizations, helplines, and reading recommendations that can guide you forward.

Each resource is offered as a potential stepping stone. No single group can cover every context, but these are recognized names or platforms that can connect you with local or specialized help. If something here isn't available in your region, consider searching for a nearby alternative ("LGBT+ center + [Your City]" or "LGBT hotline + [Your Language/Country]") or visiting a broader international organization that can point you in the right direction.

You deserve to feel supported wherever you are on your journey—whether you're navigating coming out, exploring trans identity, living with HIV, grappling with family conflict, or simply seeking like-minded community. I hope these resources shine a gentle light toward the help you need.

Mental health and crisis lines

Samaritans (International), 24/7 emotional support for anyone feeling distressed; not LGBTQ-specific, but widely used. If you can't find a local LGBTQ+ hotline, Samaritans can provide a listening ear (Phone (UK): 116 123, free 24/7). They can also direct you to local mental health resources, and their website has an international directory of crisis lines: www.samaritans.org

The Trevor Project, crisis intervention and suicide prevention for LGBTQ+ youth (up to age 24), US-based, but with some online support (Hotline (US): 1-866-488-7386). It offers real-time chats and texts, plus a community space. Even if you're slightly older than the stated age range, their website provides helpful mental health information: www.thetrevorproject.org

Trans Lifeline, peer support by and for trans people, covering crisis calls and general support (Phone (US): 1-877-565-8860; Phone (Canada): 1-877-330-6366). Even if you're not in North America, their site has helpful FAQs and can link you to local trans-friendly organizations. It is a valuable resource for trans gay men seeking peer understanding: www.translifeline.org

LGBTQ+ advocacy and community

ILGA World (International Lesbian, Gay, Bisexual, Trans, and Intersex Association) provides global updates on LGBTQ+ rights, plus a map showing where same-sex relationships or trans identities face legal barriers. Their "Member organisations" list can lead you to active local groups: www.ilga.org

Outright International works globally to document abuses against LGBTQ+ people, challenge discriminatory laws, and partner with grassroots advocates. Great for learning about legal realities or finding supportive networks in your region: www.outrightinternational.org

Stonewall, UK-based, with a global focus, offers toolkits, research, and guides on coming out, trans inclusion, and workplace policies. Though based in the UK, it has internationally relevant articles and can sometimes refer you to local allies: www.stonewall.org.uk

HIV information and support

Be in the KNOW, the successor to Avert, offers accessible, evidence-based HIV information, prevention tips, and sexual health resources: www.beintheknow.org

GMHC (Gay Men's Health Crisis), US-based, but it has comprehensive guides and resources about living with HIV. It offers educational materials on safer sex, stigma reduction, and emotional well-being for gay men. Their website may point you to sister organizations elsewhere: www.gmhc.org

UNAIDS, for worldwide data, policy updates, and practical information on prevention, treatment, and support for people living with HIV. Its website has links to local clinics and community-based organizations: www.unaids.org/en

Therapy and mental health directories

Local LGBT centers or community health clinics: Search "[Your City] + LGBT center" or "LGBT health clinic [Your

Region]." Often, these centers maintain a referral list of culturally competent therapists.

Psychology Today's therapist directory, where you can filter for "LGBTQ+-affirming," "Trans-friendly," or "HIV knowledgeable." Some countries have localized versions of this directory: www.psychologytoday.com/us/therapists

TherapyDen is similar to Psychology Today, but aims for a more inclusive listing, with specific filters for race, orientation, and issues like trauma, polyamory, etc.: www.therapyden.com

Specific communities

Black LGBTQIA+ Migrant Project (BLMP) (US): If you're navigating both racial bias and immigration issues, this group offers community-building, direct support, and advocacy tips. They may also help connect you to other identity-based groups: www.transgenderlawcenter.org/programs/blmp

Deaf Queer Resource Center, a hub for Deaf LGBTQ+ people, sharing news, cultural events, and sign-language-friendly resources: www.deafqueer.org

SAGE (Advocacy & Services for LGBTQ+ Elders) (US) has a focus on older LGBTQ+ adults—community events, housing support, phone buddies. Even if you're outside the US, they have guides relevant to older gay men's unique challenges: www.sageusa.org

If you're part of multiple communities (e.g., you're also living with HIV, or you identify as trans), exploring an organization tailored to your intersecting identities can make a big difference in feeling truly "seen."

Self-help

Books

Daring Greatly: How the Courage to Be Vulnerable Transforms the Way We Live, Love, Parent, and Lead, by Brené Brown: Not LGBTQ+-specific, but a cornerstone text on vulnerability and resilience.

The Velvet Rage: Overcoming the Pain of Growing Up Gay in a Straight Man's World, by Alan Downs: A classic on shame, validation, and healing for gay men.

Overcoming Trauma through Yoga: Reclaiming Your Body, by David Emerson and Elizabeth Hopper: For those seeking mind-body strategies to heal old wounds.

Transgender History, by Susan Stryker: Excellent for understanding trans narratives, activism, and community.

Websites for self-compassion and mindfulness

Mindful, for practical mindfulness tips and some LGBTQ+-inclusive content: www.mindful.org

Dr. Kristin Neff, Self-Compassion: https://self-compassion.org

Tips for finding local help

- *Search local directories:* If you're in a large city, there may be an LGBTQ+ center with a website listing local meetups, legal clinics, or therapy groups.

- *Check social media:* Local Facebook, Meetup, or Discord groups for LGBTQ+ folks can help you build a friend network or discover events.
- *Ask allies:* If you have one supportive health provider, counselor, or teacher, ask them for further referrals. They often have insider knowledge on specialized help.

If you're in a region with limited LGBTQ+ resources, consider:

- *Online counseling:* Many therapists offer video sessions. Make sure they're licensed and LGBTQ+-affirming.
- *Peer support communities:* Reddit (e.g., /r/lgbt, /r/asktransgender), specialized Slack or Discord servers, or small-group Zoom calls can fill gaps in local community.
- *Advocacy groups:* Reach out to bigger organizations like Outright International or ILGA for guidance on local contacts. They often maintain networks in various countries.

Closing note

No matter where you live or what hurdles you're facing, remember that these resources are stepping stones, not one-size-fits-all cures. Healing, connection, and advocacy can unfold in many ways—whether through crisis lines, consistent therapy, a caring online group, or an in-person support circle. Feel free to explore different avenues, stay curious, and lean on the compassion you've been nurturing in yourself and those around you.

You deserve respectful help. You deserve a community that sees your full identity—gay, trans, older, younger, living with HIV, Deaf, a man of color, or any intersection in between. I hope these resources serve as a welcoming light, guiding you toward the sense of belonging and affirmation that every one of us is worthy of. And if you discover new or regional resources worth sharing, consider passing them along to others—so we can keep building a more supportive world, one connection at a time.

Bibliography

Allen, A. B. and Leary, M. R. (2010) "Self-compassion, stress, and coping." *Social and Personality Psychology Compass* 4, 2, 107–118. https://doi.org/10.1111/j.1751-9004.2009.00246.x

Altman, I. and Taylor, D. A. (1973) *Social Penetration: The Development of Interpersonal Relationships*. Holt, Rinehart & Winston.

Aron, A., Aron, E. N., Tudor, M., and Nelson, G. (1991) "Close relationships as including other in the self." *Journal of Personality and Social Psychology* 60, 2, 241–253. https://doi.org/10.1037/0022-3514.60.2.241

Berridge, K. C. and Robinson, T. E. (2016) "Liking, wanting, and the incentive-sensitization theory of addiction." *American Psychologist* 71, 8, 670–679. https://doi.org/10.1037/amp0000059

Bourne, A., Reid, D., Hickson, F., Torres-Rueda, S., Steinberg, P., and Weatherburn, P. (2015) "'Chemsex' and harm reduction need among gay men in South London." *International Journal of Drug Policy* 26, 12, 1171–1176. https://doi.org/10.1016/j.drugpo.2015.07.013

Bowlby, J. (1979) "The Bowlby-Ainsworth attachment theory." *Behavioral and Brain Sciences* 2, 4, 637–638. https://doi.org/10.1017/S0140525X00064955

Bowlby, J. (1988) *A Secure Base: Parent-child Attachment and Healthy Human Development*. Basic Books. www.increaseproject.eu/images/DOWNLOADS/IO2/HU/CURR_M4-A13_Bowlby_(EN-only)_20170920_HU_final.pdf

Brennan, D. J., Crath, R., Hart, T. A., & Holtzman, S. (2017). "Body dissatisfaction and disordered eating among gay and bisexual men: The role of community norms and internalization of appearance ideals." *Journal of Gay & Lesbian Social Services*, *29*(1), 42–60. https://doi.org/10.1080/10538720.2016.1255297

Briere, J. and Scott, C. (2014) *Principles of Trauma Therapy: A Guide to Symptoms, Evaluation, and Treatment* (2nd edn). Sage Publications.

Brown, B. (2013) *Daring Greatly: How the Courage to Be Vulnerable Transforms the Way We Live, Love, Parent, and Lead*. Penguin UK.

Calabrese, S. K. and Mayer, K. H. (2020) "Stigma impedes HIV prevention by stifling patient–provider communication about U=U." *Journal of the International AIDS Society* 23, 7, e25559. https://doi.org/10.1002/jia2.25559

Calabrese, S. K., Mayer, K. H., and Marcus, J. L. (2021) "Prioritising pleasure and correcting misinformation in the era of U=U." *The Lancet HIV* 8, 3, e175–e180. https://doi.org/10.1016/s2352-3018(20)30341-6

Cloitre, M., Khan, C., Mackintosh, M.-A., Garvert, D. W., *et al.* (2019) "Emotion regulation mediates the relationship between ACES and physical and mental health." *Psychological Trauma: Theory, Research, Practice, and Policy* 11, 1, 82–89. https://doi.org/10.1037/tra0000374

Coan, J. A., Schaefer, H. S., and Davidson, R. J. (2006) "Lending a hand: Social regulation of the neural response to threat." *Psychological Science 17*, 12, 1032–1039. https://doi.org/10.1111/j.1467-9280.2006.01832.x

Downing, M. J., Schrimshaw, E. W., Scheinmann, R., Antebi, N., & Hirshfield, S. (2014). *Sexual Health, 11*(4), 388–396.

Duffy, K. A. and Chartrand, T. L. (2015) "Mimicry: Causes and consequences." *Current Opinion in Behavioral Sciences 3*, 112–116. https://doi.org/10.1016/j.cobeha.2015.03.002

Duggan, S. J. and McCreary, D. R. (2008) "Body image, eating disorders, and the drive for muscularity in gay and heterosexual men." *Journal of Homosexuality 47*, 3–4, 45–58. https://doi.org/10.1300/J082v47n03_03

Feinstein, B. A., Goldfried, M. R., and Davila, J. (2012) "The relationship between experiences of discrimination and mental health among lesbians and gay men: An examination of internalized homonegativity and rejection sensitivity as potential mechanisms." *Journal of Consulting and Clinical Psychology 80*, 5, 917–927. https://doi.org/10.1037/a0029425

Filice, E., Raffoul, A., & Meyer, S. B. (2020). "The relationship between pornography consumption and body image among gay and bisexual men: A systematic review." *Journal of Homosexuality, 67*(10), 1316–1338. https://doi.org/10.1080/00918369.2019.1609253

Frost, D. M. and Meyer, I. H. (2009) "Internalized homophobia and relationship quality among lesbians, gay men, and bisexuals." *Journal of Counseling Psychology 56*, 1, 97–109. www.ncbi.nlm.nih.gov/pmc/articles/PMC2678796

Gibson, L. E. and Leitenberg, H. (2001) "The impact of child sexual abuse and stigma on methods of coping with sexual assault among undergraduate women." *Child Abuse & Neglect 25*, 10, 1343–1361. https://doi.org/10.1016/s0145-2134(01)00279-4

Gilbert, P. (2014) "The origins and nature of compassion focused therapy." *British Journal of Clinical Psychology 53*, 6–41. doi: 10.1111/bjc.12043.

Gillath, O., Bunge, S. A., Shaver, P. R., Wendelken, C., and Mikulincer, M. (2005) "Attachment-style differences in the ability to suppress negative thoughts: Exploring the neural correlates." *NeuroImage 28*, 4, 835–847. https://doi.org/10.1016/j.neuroimage.2005.06.048

Gottman, J. M. (1999) *The Marriage Clinic: A Scientifically-Based Marital Therapy*. W. W. Norton & Company.

Gottman, J. M. (2001) *The Relationship Cure: A Five-Step Guide to Strengthening Your Marriage, Family, and Friendships*. Three Rivers Press.

Gottman, J. M. (2023) *What Predicts Divorce? The Relationship Between Marital Processes and Marital Outcomes*. (Classic edn). Routledge.

Gottman, J. M. and Silver, N. (1999) *The Seven Principles for Making Marriage Work: A Practical Guide from the Country's Foremost Relationship Expert*. (Revised edn). Harmony Books.

Gottman, J. M. and Silver, N. (2015) *The Seven Principles for Making Marriage Work: A Practical Guide from the Country's Foremost Relationship Expert*. (Revised edn.) Harmony Books.

Grubbs, J. B., Perry, S. L., Wilt, J. A., and Reid, R. C. (2018) "Pornography problems due to moral incongruence: An integrative model with a systematic review and meta-analysis." *Archives of Sexual Behavior 48*, 2, 397–425. https://doi.org/10.1007/s10508-018-1248-x

Hatzenbuehler, M. L., McLaughlin, K. A., and Xuan, Z. (2012) "Social networks and risk for depressive symptoms in a national sample of sexual minority youth." *Social Science & Medicine 75*, 7, 1184–1191. https://doi.org/10.1016/j.socscimed.2012.05.030

Hatzenbuehler, M. L., Phelan, J. C., and Link, B. G. (2013) "Stigma as a fundamental cause of population health inequalities." *American Journal of Public Health 103*, 5, 813–821. https://doi.org/10.2105/ajph.2012.301069

Herman, J. L. (1992) *Trauma and Recovery: The Aftermath of Violence—From Domestic Abuse to Political Terror*. Basic Books.

Hölzel, B. K., Carmody, J., Vangel, M., Congleton, C., *et al.* (2011) "Mindfulness practice leads to increases in regional brain gray matter density." *Psychiatry Research: Neuroimaging 191*, 1, 36–43. https://doi.org/10.1016/j.pscychresns.2010.08.006

James, S. E., Herman, J. L., Rankin, S., Keisling, M., Mottet, L., and Anafi, M. (2016) *The Report of the 2015 US Transgender Survey*. National Center for Transgender Equality.

Johnson, S. M. (2020) *The Practice of Emotionally Focused Couple Therapy: Creating Connection*. Routledge.

Katz-Wise, S. L. and Hyde, J. S. (2012) "Victimization experiences of lesbian, gay, and bisexual individuals: A meta-analysis." *Journal of Sex Research 49*, 2–3, 142–167. https://doi.org/10.1080/00224499.2011.637247

Kertzner, R. M., Meyer, I. H., Frost, D. M., and Stirratt, M. J. (2009) "Social and psychological well-being in lesbians, gay men, and bisexuals: The effects of race, gender, age, and sexual identity." *American Journal of Orthopsychiatry 79*, 4, 500–510. https://doi.org/10.1037/a0016848

Koob, G. F. and Volkow, N. D. (2016) "Neurobiology of addiction: A neurocircuitry analysis." *The Lancet Psychiatry 3*, 8, P760–773. https://doi.org/10.1016/S2215-0366(16)00104-8

Lerner, H. (2019) "Beware of apologies that won't heal." *Psychology Today*, March 20. www.psychologytoday.com/us/blog/the-dance-of-connection/201903/beware-of-apologies-that-wont-heal

Maddox, A. M., Rhoades, G. K., and Markman, H. J. (2011) "Viewing sexually explicit materials alone or together: Associations with relationship quality." *Archives of Sexual Behavior 40*, 2, 441–448. https://doi.org/10.1007/s10508-009-9585-4

Meyer, I. H. (2003) "Prejudice, social stress, and mental health in lesbian, gay, and bisexual populations: Conceptual issues and research evidence." *Psychological Bulletin 129*, 5, 674–697. https://doi.org/10.1037/0033-2909.129.5.674

Mustanski, B., Newcomb, M., and Garofalo, R. (2011) "Mental health of lesbian, gay, and bisexual youth: A developmental resiliency perspective." *Journal of Gay & Lesbian Social Services 23*, 2, 204–225. doi: 10.1080/10538720.2011.561474.

Neff, K. and Germer, C. K. (2018) *The Mindful Self-Compassion Workbook: A Proven Way to Accept Yourself, Build Inner Strength, and Thrive*. Guilford Press.

Newcomb, M. E. and Mustanski, B. (2010) "Internalized homophobia and internalizing mental health problems: A meta-analytic review." *Clinical Psychology Review 30*, 8, 1019–1029. https://doi.org/10.1016/j.cpr.2010.07.003

Pachankis, J. E., Hatzenbuehler, M. L., Rendina, H. J., Safren, S. A., and Parsons, J. T. (2015) "LGB-affirmative cognitive-behavioral therapy for young adult gay and bisexual men: A randomized controlled trial of a transdiagnostic minority stress approach." *Journal of Consulting and Clinical Psychology 83*, 5, 875–889. https://doi.org/10.1037/ccp0000037

Pachankis, J. E., Clark, K. A., Burton, C. L., Hughto, J. M. W., Bränström, R., and Keene, D. E. (2020) "Sexual orientation concealment and mental health: A conceptual and meta-analytic review." *Psychological Bulletin 146*, 5, 393–424. https://doi.org/10.1037/bul0000229

Perry, S. L. (2017) "Does viewing pornography reduce marital quality over time? Evidence from longitudinal data." *Archives of Sexual Behavior 46*, 2, 549–559. doi: 10.1007/s10508-016-0770-y.

Reis, H. T. and Shaver, P. (1988) "Intimacy as an Interpersonal Process." In S. Duck, D. F. Hay, S. E. Hobfoll, W. Ickes, and B. M. Montgomery (Eds) *Handbook of Personal Relationships: Theory, Research and Interventions* (pp.367–389). John Wiley & Sons.

Reis, H. T., Clark, M. S., and Holmes, J. G. (2004) "Perceived Partner Responsiveness as an Organizing Construct in the Study of Intimacy and Closeness." In D. J. Mashek and A. Aron (Eds) *Handbook of Closeness and Intimacy* (pp.201–225). Lawrence Erlbaum Associates.

Russell, S. T. and Fish, J. N. (2016) "Mental health in lesbian, gay, bisexual, and transgender (LGBT) youth." *Annual Review of Clinical Psychology 12*, 1, 465–487. https://doi.org/10.1146/annurev-clinpsy-021815-093153

Ryan, C., Russell, S. T., Huebner, D., Diaz, R., and Sanchez, J. (2010) "Family acceptance in adolescence and the health of LGBT young adults." *Journal of Child and Adolescent Psychiatric Nursing 23*, 4, 205–213. https://doi.org/10.1111/j.1744-6171.2010.00246.x

Salter Ainsworth, M. D., Blehar, M. C., Waters, E., and Wall, S. (1978) *Patterns of Attachment: A Psychological Study of the Strange Situation*. Lawrence Erlbaum Associates.

Schore, A. N. (2001) "Effects of a secure attachment relationship on right brain development, affect regulation, and infant mental health." *Infant Mental Health Journal 22*, 1–2, 7–66. https://doi.org/10.1002/1097-0355(200101/04)22:1%3C7::aid-imhj2%3E3.0.co;2-n

Sewell, J., Cambiano, V., Miltz, A., Speakman, A., *et al.* (2018) "Changes in recreational drug use, drug use associated with chemsex, and HIV-related behaviours, among HIV-negative men who have sex with men in London and Brighton, 2013–2016." *Sexually Transmitted Infections 94*, 7. https://sti.bmj.com/content/94/7/494

Siegel, D. J. (2007) *The Mindful Brain: Reflection and Attunement in the Cultivation of Well-Being*. W.W. Norton & Company.

Simpson, J. A. and Rholes, W. S. (2017) "Adult attachment, stress, and romantic relationships." *Current Opinion in Psychology 13*, 19–24. doi: 10.1016/j.copsyc.2016.04.006.

Sabin, J. A., Riskind, R. G., and Nosek, B. A. (2015) "Health care providers' implicit and explicit attitudes toward lesbian women and gay men." *American Journal of Public Health 105*, 9, 1831–1841. https://doi.org/10.2105/AJPH.2015.302631

Stewart-Williams, S., & Thomas, A. G. (2013). "The ape that thought it was a peacock: Does evolutionary psychology contribute anything to the debate on pornography and sexual violence?" *Review of General Psychology*, *17*(3), 235–247. https://doi.org/10.1037/a0033047

Stuart, D. (2019) "Chemsex: Origins of the word, a history of the phenomenon and a respect to the culture." *Drugs and Alcohol Today 19*, 1, 3–10. https://doi.org/10.1108/DAT-10-2018-0058

Terrence Higgins Trust (2018) *The Chemsex Care Plan: A Guide for Men Who Have Sex with Men Engaging in Chemsex*. www.tht.org.uk/our-work/sexual-health/chemsex

Terrence Higgins Trust (2021) "Chemsex: Information and support." www.tht.org.uk

The Trevor Project (2021) *The Trevor Project's 2021 National Survey on LGBTQ Youth Mental Health*. www.thetrevorproject.org/survey-2021

Tomkins, A., George, R., & Kliner, M. (2019). *BMJ Open*, *9*(7), e030505.

Volkow, N. D., Wang, G.-J., Fowler, J. S., Tomasi, D., and Telang, F. (2011) "Addiction: Beyond dopamine reward circuitry." *Proceedings of the National Academy of Sciences 108*, 37, 15037–15042. https://doi.org/10.1073/pnas.1010654108

Wagenmakers, E. J., Morey, R. D., and Lee, M. D. (2016) "Bayesian benefits for the pragmatic researcher." *Current Directions in Psychological Science 25*, 3, 169–176. https://doi.org/10.1177/0963721416643289

Willoughby, B. J., Carroll, J. S., & Busby, D. M. (2016). "Differences in pornography use among couples: Associations with relationship and sexual satisfaction." *Journal of Sex Research*, *53*(6), 678–689. https://doi.org/10.1080/00224499.2015.1051481

Wright, P. J., Tokunaga, R. S., & Kraus, A. (2016). "A meta-analysis of pornography consumption and actual sexual behavior." *Journal of Communication*, *66*(1), 183–205. https://doi.org/10.1111/jcom.12201

Wright, P. J., Tokunaga, R. S., and Kraus, A. (2016) "Consumption of pornography, perceived peer norms, and condomless sex." *Health Communication 31*, 8, 954–963. doi: 10.1080/10410236.2015.1022936.

